The
PRIVATE EYE
Book of
CRAIG BROWN
PARODIES

For Rupert and Anya Forbes Adam
and in Memory of Peter Cook

Published in Great Britain by
Private Eye Productions Ltd.,
6 Carlisle Street, London W1V 5RG
in association with Corgi Books.

©1995 Pressdram Ltd. ISBN 0 552 14403 7

Designed by Bridget Tisdall.
Cover photograph by Graham Trott
Printed in England by
Ebenezer Baylis & Son Ltd, Worcester.

Corgi Books are published by Transworld Publishers Ltd 61–
63 Uxbridge Road, Ealing, London W5 5SA
in Australia by Transworld Publishers (Australia) Pty, Ltd 15–
23 Helles Avenue, Moorebank, NSW 2170
and in New Zealand by Transworld Publishers (N.Z.) Ltd 3
William Pickering Drive, Albany, Auckland.
2 4 6 8 10 9 7 5 3 1

The

PRIVATE EYE

Book of
CRAIG BROWN
PARODIES

PRIVATE EYE • CORGI

Foreword by
JEFFREY ARCHER

As a fellow writer — and one not unknown for his keen sense of humour! — I am delighted to have been asked to introduce this slim volume of Craig Brown's Parodies.

It is now getting on for a decade since I became Editor-in-Chief of *Private Eye* magazine. In that time the world has witnessed many changes.

On a personal level, my achievements have indeed been heartening.

As Chairman of the Conservative Party I have successfully steered us past the winning post in two General Elections.

In my role as captain of the English Cricket team, I have taken pride in our five consecutive Test victories.

As an author, I am delighted to say my books now outsell all others in the world apart from the Bible. I am confidently informed that my latest is a strong contender for the Prix Goncourt, which will complete a personal Hat Trick of last year's Booker Prize (1994) and the year before's Nobel Prize for Literature (1993).

And as the lead singer of "Take That!", I have led the group straight into the Number One slot in the pop charts on no less than seven different occasions.

Not bad! Not bad at all!

Like many other "over-achievers", I like to relax from time to time by putting my feet up with a glass of chilled white wine and a thumping good read. And this book is certainly that. Well done.

I'm sorry to say this but it came as some surprise to me that the publishers have chosen to call it *"The Private Eye Book of Craig Brown Parodies"*. Not that I am saying for one minute that Craig Brown didn't write them, merely that my own part in their creation — up to 90% at a rough guestimate — has gone unacknowledged.

Like the Prime Minister, the President of the United States, the Pope and David Mellor — ask him — Craig Brown is a close personal friend of mine. And every fortnight I have come to expect his call, regular as clockwork.

"Jeffrey, old man — having a spot of trouble — the words don't seem to be flowing — could you possibly write this one for me — just this once — ever so grateful". I can honestly say I know his patter back-to-front!

But he's a mate, and I like to help any mate in a fix. So being a bit of softie and a bloke who's not in the least bit frightened of old-fashioned hard work, I dutifully trot out the required parody for *Private Eye*.

Fine.

But would the courtesy of the smallest acknowledgement really have been asking too much? Even those two little words "thank you" wouldn't have gone amiss, you know, Craig!

Mind you, as a past Governor of the Bank of England, I have learnt it's not worth losing a minute's sleep over the might-have-beens. So I take these disappointments in my stride.

I wish this little book all the luck in the world. And, talking of the world, did you know I was the first man to make a solo circumnavigation of the world in a ketch?

But that's another story! All the best!

Cap Ferrat • Rio de Janeiro • Aspen • Munich.
Aug-Oct 1995

MARTIN AMIS

What happens when galaxies collide? When galaxies collide what happens? What *happens* when galaxies collide? This is the mega-question, you know: *galaxies having collided, happens what*?

That's the gammily effluent inquisitorial presupposition — the *question* — that rocks and tosses — never flosses, not *now* — the veined and corpuscled American football in my skull the neuro-surgeons know as my brain, intricated as a spider's web of phlegm, though disappointingly less tasty.

The speed of light is 186,282 mps and one light hour is 670,000,000 miles. This means that when "Martin Amis"— not me, but "Martin Amis" — is yearningly staring at the mug-reflector on the ceiling at night (when men cry) and he sees two blackheads — headblacks — protruding from his cheeks like hooded negroes on the prowl and he loftily squeezes them and pounds them and knocks them about and they squirt their tears of pus skywards, and there's a hollow-caustic mess on the mug reflector, he takes a few seconds to see it. And that's what happens when galaxies collide. When galaxies collide, *that's* what happens.

Interviews, interviews and more interviews, they come like blow-jobs in the scuzzy London night, (when men cry). They're all after me: the *Sunday Times*, the *Standard*, the *New Dentician*, *The Scotsman*, *Molars Gazette*, *Gums Illustrated*, *Options*, *The London Review of Teeth*, *Maclean's Quarterly*, *Esquire*, *Just Fillings*, *The International Root Canal Observer*, and the *Reader's Digest*, which wants to run extracts.

They all freaked out over the book, and wanted to know more about it, like when I was writing it, did my teeth already ache, or did they begin to hurt afterwards, and whether I use a pen or a pencil for getting at those awkward bits in between, and what my daily routine as a significant novelist is — rinse, brush, rinse, or just brush and rinse, three times a day or just twice, and where exactly do I stand on toothpicks? No book has ever received more attention, not since the Big Bang, when the earth blew up like a pulsing snotrag.

My normal day, huh? First, I grunge the sicky-wicky, then I scowze out the scab-tube, then I skunk down the flunk-pustule, and that just about takes me up to lunch. For lunch, I'll have a light shit-snack of cannelloni with tomato sauce like the castrated cocks of two hundred dwarves dowsed in their own blood, then its back to irking the scuzz-wock. Then I'll screw-whack the scrag-head and soil the downside of the whinge-pussy before getting in a bit of shagbagging the apothegm before a dinner of Supa-scrag-fleck-on-toast. After dinner, it's down to the spick-arse to sconse some clap-wax off a pluto-gasket, and then its into my jim-jams and nighty-night with heads down for beddy-byes.

This is the big one, it's the zoom-race, the mega-smegma-marathon, the outface-olympiad of inky guys who knock each other out every single bloody day with pen-punches to the chin. I'm talking books. Those things. And I'm talking novelists. Big novelists. Who's up there with me? In this scrawny little country, no-one touches me, no-one comes near. *Not anyone*. No way, ho-zay. On the spinning roulette-globe of posterity I'm up there with the mega-Americans, and I've got written confirmation, solid as a brick through your window in the night (when men cry), from the real big guys, like Bellow and Updike. Like, on the beigey backside of my latest, *The Information*, there's quotes — *quotes* — from both those guys, and see them *salivate*.

"Martin Amis is attempting to have a go at trying to construct a new sort of book not all that different from a novel" — JOHN UPDIKE.

"Martin Amis certainly uses words. Our greatest writers have also used words. And with enough of those words placed in the right order, you find you have written a book. Martin Amis has written a book, or books, and that's pretty heady. It places him outside the central tradition of fishmongers, ball-bearing salesmen and fire chiefs, few of whom have achieved such a thing" — SAUL BELLOW.

See?

I am the rat-nosed novelist of urban decay, sniffing out insights into the metropolitan uranus amongst the skunky puddles of the city (where men cry at night) as it fist-fucks its way to the murkily alopeciac millennium. But now I've been paid a sum commensurate with my skills, I am in the position of having the urban decay sent up to me, rather than having to go out and look for it myself.

Yesterday, I started on my new book, on my new book I started. Yesterday. That's what I started on: my new book. I'm paid per sentence, these days. Paid. Per. Sentence. These. Days. Repetitions included. And repetitions are included too. Anywozzle, I want to hunt out some new territory, to take this new novel, this new page-clump, in a really major new direction, a take-breathing new departure for a novelist at the very peek-a-boo of his capabilities. So I hit upon this great new theme, previously untackled by any novelist. Death. Death, and the way we're all getting older, and we're all going to die, and *no-one but me, the novelist "Martin Amis", realises it*. I brain-thought it'd be mega-cool to mix this theme in with another brilliant new theme: urban decay. So I had my bloke nip down to the streets with a check-list I'd supplied, with instructions to bring back: 1) a dog turd, 2) a half-eaten potato chip, 3) A noisy pop record, 4) a used oozily vivacious elastoplast, 5) A black man called something suitably absurd, 6) a scoop of something unashamedly glutinous. I'm now waiting for his return with the six, bitch-biro in my hand, so I can splat them down in my incandescent prose as quick as possible before sending him back out onto the rucky streets with them all. Now all I — "Martin Amis" have to do is conjure up a brand new character to go with them — a sort of Keith Talent/Richard Tull, John Self sort of character, but kind of different, may-be and, together with my unique insights into astronomy, I should be able to create a pretty intoxicating new snot-Bible for the viscid depression of the new millennium. Pretty sophisticated; pretty scrunge-bummy, huh?

ROSEANNE ARNOLD

You know what, I don't give a shit. I don't give a shit about the crap, and, like, I don't give a crap about the shit. I stand for the victim. In my show, the Woman is no longer a victim, but in control of her own mind. With "Roseanne" I'm, like, revolutionising the whole goddamn structure of corporate America, I'm saying, right, you take all the pain and the fear and the *truth* of what it's like to be a poor woman with a family in America, and you put them on that fucking screen, dickhead. And that's, like, how "Roseanne" has come to stand for creative freedom and freedom for women and freedom for *reality* in America. Scenes like this one may have made the moguls and executives spend two hours of their lives shitting pink, but I'm telling you they've liberated American women and that counts far more to me than any goddamn thing, so kiss my ass:

Roseanne: Jeez, I, like, slopped coffee over my dress.
Dan: This chair's kinda broke. I just fell off it!
Roseanne: That makes me real mad. Hey, I just smashed a cup.
Becky: Don't get mad, mom.
Dan: No, don't get mad, hon.
Roseanne: Like, why the goddamn not?
Dan and Becky: 'Cos we love you, Roseanne.
Roseanne: Aw, shucks. And I guess I kinda love the both of you too.

(Laughter and applause)

Let no one kid you that kind of scene comes easy 'cause sure as hell it don't. I employed fifteen different writers on that first line alone, and they worked their butts off for seventy-two hours without sleeping, like, with me coming and screaming: "You know what? You're all talentless bags of shit who ought to be kissing my ass for me allowing you to write on my show. 'Cause none of you have any goddamn talent. What kind of a dickass line is this: 'Jeez, I, like, slopped coffee over my *blouse*'? What the fuck do you tweedy little asses know about *real life*? None of you ever lived in a goddamned *trailer*, you screwasses! Roseanne doesn't wear a goddamn *blouse*. You better pack your goddamn bags 'cause if you don't come up with something better than a *blouse* you're gonna be out on the street, assholes."

I prefer to deal with them like that, because my psychiatrist says I've got to overcome my deep instinctive nonconfrontational impulses, inflicted on me by a bullying male-dominated society. So, like, after another twenty four hours the fifteen of 'em came up with:

Roseanne: Jeez, I, like, slopped coffee over my *dress*.

And, like, I was pretty goddamn thrilled, 'cause that's a really great line, so to celebrate and to tell them I loved them I went into their room and I sacked only five of them. And, like, you should have seen the look on the faces of the other ten: they were just so fucking *grateful* they even smiled at me.

I am a gust of wind
Looking for a leaf to blow
I am a silvery cloud
Scudding over the horizon
In search of calm repose
I am a soul struggling to
regain
itself
From the oceans
of
despair
and
I'll like kick the shit out of your fucking
dickhead asses you talentless fucking pricks
if you fail
to agree
with
me.

My fight, my battle, is the fight, the battle, for all women, everywhere, for all women who are sick to hell of the language of war and aggression employed by male society. And my fight is for women to stand up for themselves.

I make that pretty goddamn plain in immortal dialogue from "Roseanne" everyone in the world remembers like:

Roseanne: I'm not gonna do the washing-up today. You do the goddamn washing-up for once, I'm, like, sick of it.
Becky: Love ya, mom.
Roseanne: Jeez, hon, guess I went a bit wild just now. Love you, too. Heck, I got a swell idea — let's just like leave the washin-up 'til tomorrow and have ourselves a beer!

(Laughter and applause)

I want women everywhere to be treated with the respect denied them for centuries by the ego-centred male. So I get pretty sicked-off when other women, fat-assed bitches who could piss acid through their noses, don't treat me with the respect I, as Woman, deserve. Like, last fall a woman, a goddamned dung-eating tumorous piece of shit, comes up to me on an airplane — and remember she wasn't even *permitted* in first class — and says, like, "Roseanne, I'm your number one fan, can I kindly have your autograph, please?" like as if the world owed her a living. So, I was like, Jesus, what am I gonna do, I'm like a child again, I can't handle it, like you wake up and there's this fat bitch asking for your auto, so, hell, like I guess I care too much, I completely regressed, so I say to Tom, that's my husband, get her goddamn outta here, and he stands up to the bitch and says, like, do you want me to drag you by the neck outside and beat the crap outta you? And we never hear another word from her. I hope this teaches women like me to stand on their own two feet, to kick ass, and not to take shit from goddamned anyone, right? As my therapist has taught me to say to myself each day as I arise, I am not a victim, nor will I ever be. And that goes for all goddamned victims, everywhere.

I'd like to thank the following for helping me write this diary. Love ya. There were times when it felt like it was so much unmitigated pain, like I was pulling my heart out with both hands and eating it with my mouth, and then regurgitating it and eating it again only this time having lost my teeth. But I got through it, I took all my pain and suffering and hurt and turned it into a really beautiful son, and for this I thank:

My doctors.
My kids.
My psychotherapists.
My dolls.
My razorblades.
My analyst.
All the people within me.
My talent.
My tremendous compassion.
My overdeveloped sense of justice.
My obsessive need to care.
The plain ordinary working woman within me who's still trying to scratch a living to provide food for her family.

TONY BENN MP

Tuesday April 13th, 1995. Let's keep personalities out of it. Let's stick to the issues. That's been the abiding belief of my political life these past fifty-five years, and I intend to stick to it in this diary. Harold wouldn't have agreed with keeping personalities out of it, of course. Oh no, not Harold. Though it's on record that I always found him on a personal basis a very nice man, Harold was always ruthless in his dealings with his ministers, and often two-faced and deceitful, stubborn, unprincipled and frankly on a personal basis rather unpleasant.

And what of this new chap, Blair? John tells me that Roy told him that Brian once heard from Rodney that this new fellow Campbell was rumoured to have told Margaret Beckett that Bill thought John's view of Blair was something completely unprintable. I also have it on very good authority — from Jim via Jack through Bernie, who heard it from someone in the T&G at last year's Conference — that Blair prefers personalities and what I call tittle-tattle to the cut-and-thrust of democratic debate.

Wednesday April 14th, 1995. Funny, isn't it, the way the Establishment, through the press barons of the multinational media, in conjunction with their foreign paymasters, is still dead set on undermining me, personally and politically, by making me out to be somehow "paranoid"? What absolute tosh they talk — as though I'm some sort of mad-eyed "conspiracy theorist"!!! But this is all part of a closely-orchestrated capitalist campaign to destroy me, and through me the political will of the British people. It serves the Establishment's political and commercial interests, doesn't it, to make me out as some sort of "obsessive" character! Of course, nothing could be further from the truth, as the archive of tape-recordings, memos, diaries, notes, letters, speeches and draft amendments I have stored away these past fifty-five years make absolutely crystal clear.

Thursday April 15th 1995. It happened again this morning. I had just finished tape-recording myself for the archives, swallowing my third mug of tea and finishing off a banana fruit when the newspapers — many of them still delivered by workers to the private homes of millionaires, even in this day and age! — were delivered to my home. What, I wondered, are the latest press comments about me and the democratic policies I have been fighting for tooth and nail these past fifty years? I read every page of the Daily Express, including sports and arts, into the tape recorder, but, on my playback, failed to hear a single mention of myself and my policies.

It's their new strategy, y'see. Having in the past sought to undermine democracy by lampooning me they now try to achieve the same result by ignoring me, making me out to be some sort of "fringe" character!

Poured myself another cup of tea. The tape-recorder picked up all the glugs, so it obviously doesn't need new batteries quite yet.

Friday April 16th, 1995. Have found a way of knotting my necktie using an extraordinary little gadget on my Swiss Army penknife. Its recommended use in the accompanying pamphlet is for taking the stones out of horses' hooves, but they keep these other uses quiet, don't they, just in case the ordinary decent people get to hear of them. Whereas tying me necktie used to take, ooh, a minute, with this handy gadget it can now take over 15 minutes. I can't recommend it enough. Of course, the minute word gets out about it, it'll be dynamite, and there'll be the most massive international cover-up involving all the powers the state has at its disposal. But that's what you'd expect of the feudal hierarchy under which we are forced to live, isn't it? Either that, or they make one out to be potty!

Unpeel a banana fruit and eat it, first throwing away the mushy white bit inside.

Saturday April 17th, 1995. I have two tape-recorders, one newer and more capable, the other older and rather more experienced. For security reasons, I don't often leave them in a room together, but I have often wondered how they behave when they are alone. So simply by way of experiment, I placed the two of them together in my office having first — quite unknown to them — placed a third tape-recorder in an upper drawer of my desk with the "Record" button pressed on.

The results are fascinating. For three hours, not a single murmur from either of them. Or were they tipped off by the third tape-recorder, as a result of some sort of nod-and-wink from the powers that be? I'll investigate further next week. A fourth tape-recorder may well be needed.

Sunday April 18th 1995. Whatever faults I may have as a politician, if any, I can honestly say that throughout the course of my political life, I have been a man of the strongest principle. That's something not even my closest political allies would wish to contradict. Let's not beat about the bush. The strength of my principles is such that, time and time again, I came very close to resigning from the Callaghan government. For instance, I bitterly disagreed with Jim and the rest of the Cabinet over incomes policy, defence, Europe, Northern Ireland and crawling cap-in-hand to the IMF. I frequently said: "Frankly Jim, I'm not going to take it any more, my principles won't let me. I have

no choice but to resign". But — and this I may say is typical Jim — he always managed to avoid being in the room whenever I made these threats.

But at least one of us maintained his principles to the end. Speaking as the British people, I am proud to have emerged from five years of Labour Government with my conscience intact. It meant that I could roundly rebuke those of my fellow Ministers who meekly gave way on these vital public issues, shamefully hanging on to political office at any cost. I had no time for such hypocrisy.

Monday April 19th 1995. Interesting, isn't it, the way it's now all Blair, Blair, Blair. The media are building him up as some sort of future leader of the Labour Party, trying to isolate myself and the broad mass of the working people of this country from the source of real democratic power. But I have faith in the British people. I have absolute trust in the ballot box, just so long as the right people are called on to vote. From the historic perspective, I am convinced that it can't be long before the workers secure for themselves the common ownership of the means of prod prod prod prod prod. Blow me down, something wrong with the old tape-recorder. Best leave it to soak overnight in water, and resume recording tomorrow.

THE RT HON VIRGINIA BOTTOMLEY MP

If you'll just let me finish... it's always a tremendous morale-booster to be at the launch of a major new Health Service promotion, setting out in the clearest possible terms the achievements and progress springing from the bold new initiatives being undertaken by our Department.

Last week saw the launch of our 'Get Up and Go' video package for the terminally ill, which showed that, under our important new 'ADIOS' scheme, up to 48% of all first-time mortalities are now being allowed to pass away peacefully in the comfort of their own homes, and a further 86% are being treated by a skilled operative — in the vast majority of cases a trained funeral director — within just 48 hours of their permanent cessation. Figures also show that 93% of our patients are beginning to enjoy death much more, with up to 47% at any one time maintaining that they have either quite enjoyed or very much enjoyed their last few minutes, and a further 82% saying that, given

the choice, they were glad to have breathed their last in the warmth and comfort of a hospital corridor rather than under the sometimes traumatic conditions of the operating theatre. This must be good news for us all, and recent surveys undertaken by our Department suggest that up to 42% of hospital corridors at any one time offer warm, caring environments to at least eight corpses, and that a further 93% of these corpses look either "quite cheerful" or "very cheerful indeed". This all rather makes me think that a jolly good pat on the department back from some elements in the media may be long overdue!

Virginia Says: Devolving responsibility to the consumer constitutes a major initiative. Do please save time and trouble by performing minor hip replacement surgery in the comfort of your own home. A sharp knife, a couple of safety pins and a clean set of garden tools should do the trick, saving our Health Service the countless millions we desperately need to spend on costly cutbacks and bold money-saving initiatives.

Not long now until our celebrated annual Bottomley clan holiday get-together on the Isle of Wight, with all the organisation and reorganisation involved. It's always a simple, family affair, but as I say on my seaside postcards, a decent holiday is all about having the courage to devolve responsibility whilst keeping a tight grip on overall budgetary requirements.

The statistics of the Bottomley family seaside initiative are really quite staggering: four great uncles (including the celebrated Cambridge croupier Benjamin Bottomley), three great aunts (among them the distinguished Conservative thinker Lavinia Lobottomey), twelve nephews and nieces (including a regional Pickastix champion and two Blue Peter badge holders), eight cousins (among them a senior newscaster and prime-site dental hygienist), three Jays, five Crows and eight Wrens, ten television camera crews, fifteen still photographers, twenty print journalists, a senior branch manager from good old Marks and Spencer plus accompanying fitters, two press officers from the Department of Health, a variety of catering vans for the media and, of course, my own immediate family, in statistical accordance with department projections, comprising one son, two daughters and my devoted husband Peter the backbencher, he's sweet.

And all for an ice-lolly in a straw hat on the beach at 1100 hours before an immediate return to the Department by noon for seasonal reduction of organisational overload! Sometimes I think it's hardly worth it — but then I consider the very real pleasure those beaming photos of generations of Bottomleys give to so many millions of Britons, and — call me a big softie — I simply cannot say "no"! Tremendous fun!

Virginia Says: Never forget your photographer when visiting a hospital — there may always be a patient who can manage a smile.

Despite what the media would like to have us think, I find that ordinary Britons up and down the country continue to have great faith in our Health Service. Let me give you an example, if you'll let me finish.

Last week, as I was opening a new bulldozer, an old woman came up to me. "Mrs Bottomley," she said, tears in her eyes, "I'd like to thank you for all you've done for our local hospital. It was the most terrible eyesore blocking out our lovely view and luckily I'm on BUPA."

These and many millions of other heartwarming tales concerning the success of the Government's Health Initiatives are told to me regularly by ordinary, decent Britons. So why, may I ask, are they never reported in the media?

Virginia Says: Tests show that excessive use of alcohol and tobacco is no longer a problem among the deeply infirm and recently deceased. I think the rest of us could jolly well learn something from their example, don't you?

Many years ago, I joined the Conservative Party and if you'll let me finish I'll tell you why. I joined the Conservative Party because I *cared*. I *cared* about the massive amounts of ordinary taxpayers' money being thrown at other people's problems, I *cared* about reducing overheads in our Health Service, I *cared* that our doctors and nurses were getting a raw deal and I *knew* that only through cutting their workload by reducing the numbers of patients would we find ourselves in a position to lay them off in any great numbers.

Sometimes I look at myself in the mirror and I hear people say to me, "Virginia, your trouble is that you care too much — you really should be more ambitious". But frankly I'm not the ambitious type — after all, if I were really ambitious, I'd be prime minister by now, and not just in seven to eight years time.

Virginia Says: I visited a lovely, lovely old gentleman in hospital the other day, a really thoroughly smashing old boy. "Give us a glass of water, Virginia, love — I'm dying," he joked, a twinkle in his eye, while the photographer was reloading his camera. "Why not get in touch with your local water company?" I explained, caringly. He'd obviously never heard about our super new emphasis on the devolution of responsibility to the consumer, so I pressed our new "Away with You" Health Service pamphlet into his hand. He died later that night, and, do you know, he had read it all the way through! Just one of the many lovely caring success stories from today's revitalised Department of Health, working 24 hours a day, 365 days a year, just to make my world a better place.

JULIE BURCHILL

Phew — what a bloody relief!

A week's gone by without a word from so-called Prince Wills. Not forgetting that tiny-teetotal-four-foot-zero-inches twerp Prince Harry.

What a pair. What a paltry, po-faced, perpetually photo-opportunising, pansyish, poxyish pair!

To look at them, you might think that half a pound of Anchor wouldn't melt in their mealy mouths. But frankly you'd be R-O-N-G. No — you can't come the innocents with me, you little shorts-wearing, side-partinged, sandal-sporting, scummy little schemers.

From the start, Harry and Wills have been up to their necks in this scandal.

And you can't tell me they ain't.

Whoah! When the English Royal Family finally disappears down the plughole to join the Bay City Rollers and Wayne Fontana in Oblivion City, it's those piss-awful Princes Harry and Wills the finger will be pointing at.

Have you ever noticed how their eyes are too close together?

Yet those sycophantic and slimy schoolboy Cyclopses ponce about as if they were God's own gift to womanhood.

Well, let's spell it out so they can hear; frankly, I'd rather go on a blind date with a used teabag than find myself in the cot with Harry or Wills.

So put that in your By Appointment pipes and smoke it, schoolboys.

Bosnia, Schmosnia.

You-go-slav — I'll follow.

Frankly, those Bosnians make Madonna look like Morrisey after he's listened to an all-night session by The Shamen — and that's saying something!

England's a bloody brilliant place to live in compared to Yugoslavia. We've got Princess Di. The Groucho. Nintendo. And Me.

So why does everyone go on about Yugoslavia as if it was some kind of really great TV show like The Generation Game used to be before the piss-awful Larry Grayson, a kind of rich man's Vaclav Havel, took over?

And not content with yak-yakking about the Yucky Yugos for as long as the average Pink Floyd Concept Album — yawnsville! — now we're going to send them bloody Aid!

What I say is: why not send them Aids instead and be done with it!

Or if we've got to parachute parcels on the Batey Bosnians, let's make sure we wrap Harry and Wills up in 'em first!

Now there's a thought!

So bloody what if some bloke's goin' round cutting the dongs off gee-gees?

Good for him!

What have horses ever done for civilisation? 'That's what I'd like to know. Where's the great gee-gee novelist? The great gee-gee philosopher? And no horse I can think of has its own million-pound column on a mass-market Sunday newspaper.

All they've given us in the entire history of civilisation is the Horse of the Year Show — talk about instant switch-off — and 'Flipper'.

And Flipper wasn't even a horse. He was a bloody Dolphin.

But the English have always been soft on horses. Pathetic, really, when you think that a dobbin is only a sort of mis-shapen dog with a big nose, a neigh and more fleas.

And, talking of dogs, they get in the way, too.

Personally, I'd like to de-dong all dogs, fry all goldfish, Kastrate all Kitties and eat every last bloody horse in the country between two slices of bread. And as for cuddly little hamsters, can't they find anything better to do than run around wheels all day? Frankly, I'd like to send them all to Kelloggs and have them made into Hammy Pop-Tarts.

And as for dolphins — if they're so good at talking, then you name me a single dolphin *anywhere in the world* with his own chatshow. You can't?

'Nuff said.

So what's so bad about serial-killers?

From the way the poncey, pass-the-Petrus, Puccini-playing Hampstead Unintelligentsia are bleating on about it, you'd think there was something wrong — daahling — about clocking up more homicides than Mick Jagger has had hot dinners.

So these lily-livered, limp-wristed, Lorca-loving lettuce-heads gather in their swanky swagged-and-ruched sitting-rooms served by a smorgasbord of Sicilian servants to tut-a-tut-tut to one another about how SIMPLY AWWWFUL it was of Jeff Dahmer and Dirty Den Nilsen to kiss-'n'-kill.

Pardon me while I puke.

At least Jeff'n'Den never bored us with their *South Bank Shows* and their piss-poor Booker-shortlisted state-of-Britain novels and their *Late Show* yawnathons.

At least they never grew manky moustaches like so-called President Vacant Havel.

At least they never received Brit Awards.

And at least they never sipped Pina Coladas with Mick Hucknall at Stringfellows.

So let's get this straight, shall we?

If it isn't "Dahmer for President" in 1996, then the United States of Amoronica will be shown as even more pathetic than I thought it was already.

And if the Tories are looking for a tough, single-minded successor to Mr Un-Major, there's only one thing for it.

Vote Nilsen.

Suddenly the whole world seems to be talking about just one subject.

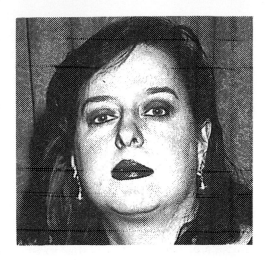

ME.

Makes you think, eh? What an amazingly brill achievement! You know one thing? I'm the first working-class girly in the history of the whole bloody universe to have her own highly paid — we're talking **billions** a year — column on a mega-brill paper. Except for Lynda Lee-Potter, that is. And Jean Rook. And Marje Proops, and — oh, anyway, I'm the only person in the history of England who's been able to make zillions out of mega-great supa-brill schlockbusters, full of sex, drugs and slavery and at the same time write full-length serious novels what show just how intelligent and artistic I is.

Just like what that mega-groovy grandad Graham Greene did.

So when's my full-length serious novel coming out?

When I've written it!

And what's it going to be about?

It's going to be about 200 pages long, big type, no pix, author's name — JULIE BURCHILL — in gold.

And it's going to be about what a serious writer I am — more serious than Morrisey and Kafka and Prince and Nietzsche and Princess Di put together!

So stuff you, pixie pratfaces Princes Harry and Wills — Burchill's gonna be bigger than the both of you — so there!

ALAN CLARK

Bumped into a ghastly little woman at reception the other night. Took her to be one of the waitresses: common as muck, foreign look about her, nasal voice, not a bad bust, decidedly alluring to be frank, tidy-poo hairdo, had her marked down as a cleaning lady, obviously fancied me something rotten, kept giving me the come-on by asking me questions of the "What exactly is it that you do, ooh that must be interesting" variety.

Was just plotting to offer her tuppence ha'penny an hour to clean out the stables when I suddenly found myself getting the hots for her. Must have been her feet — two of 'em, one on each side, quite small, well shod, not bad at all. So I put my arm round her shoulder, volunteered her my broadest grin, and whispered into her ear, "If you really want to know EXACTLY what I do, why don't we bunk up together for a few mins in a little Ministerial cupboard I spotted out in the corridor — let me 'Minister' to your every urge, know what I mean, hur, hur?"

At this point, an oik in pin-stripes sidled over to the cleaning lady and said, "Your Majesty, may I present Lady Someone-or-other?" Crikey, I thought, how utterly spastic of me — I've been trying to have it off with the Queen. Smack botties for Alan. Silly really, because I hardly ever fancy Krauts: no sense of humour. Mind you, if my memory serves, I rather think I had it away with that daughter of hers, Anne Thingummyjig, some time in the late 70s, bit of a boot face but quite a goer, and Margaret's quite a pole-vaulter, of course, and that Fergie looks a lot of fun in a tarty way, and Princess Michael could f**k the hind legs off a grand piano, even if she is a bit of a nouve, and of origin unknown.

On the way to the Ministry, spotted a blind man plus begging bowl. Bit of a moral dilemma, but I finally removed the money from the begging bowl, stuck my tongue out at him and gave him a bloody good kick in the shins. Felt a bit of a s**t, who wouldn't, etcetera, but what other options were open to one? I simply felt in all honesty I had to teach him a thing or two. This is the real world. It's no good all these snotty little liberal buggers getting on their high horses about this sort of decisive action if they can't come up with a halfway decent alternative. Lucky the poor bugger wasn't a blind woman, or it wouldn't only have been my tongue that I stuck out, arf arf!!

Saw that fat loathsome incompetent oaf Ken Clarke. "Lovely to see you Ken," I said, "You're doing marvellously at the Home Office. Highly impressive. Keep it up."

"Jolly nice of you to say so, Alan," he replied, sick-makingly.

What a first-class hypocrite! What an utter five-star shit! The slimy toad must have known I didn't believe a word I was saying. Yet without so much as blinking he came out with utter crap, piss and balls like: "Jolly nice of you to say so, Alan."

What a lying git! How pukey can you get? And how spassy and nouveau of him to think I wouldn't see through it! Who does he think I am?

Talking of ratbags, that Dalai Lama's a prize shit, oily and loathsome little creep of the first order, awful churchy holier-than-thou-air about him.

"What's your game then, baldie?" I said to him when we met at a parliamentary reception back in '89.

"Velly nice meety you," he replied.

"Cut the cackle," I said. "Just tell me why you insist on poncing about like a prize ninny in those godawful robes. Who'd you think you are? Mrs Gertrude Shilling?"

"Solly, no understandy," he answered.

What a sanctimonious little charlatan, all smiles and deep bows and sweaty hands clasped together in prayer, talking nonstop balls. Nouve, too: no gentleman ever wears orange. I could see through him a mile off. "I can see YOU never went to Eton!" I said — and that saw him off pretty damn quick.

At an opportune moment, I took Margaret Thatcher — never lovelier, good uplift to her bra, under-rated B.T.M. too, oozing with controlled sexuality — to one side. "See the little bloke over there, Margaret," I whispered. "Definitely not to be trusted. Been talking the most frightful gibberish about loving thy neighbour, learning to live together, not killing each other and similar complete balls. I think he must be up to something."

"But who can we trust these days, Alan?" said Margaret, using my first name — a sure sign that a woman's trying to lure one under a table for a quick one-two.

I took the bull by the horns. "Personally, Margaret, I've always thought Saddam Hussein seriously under-rated, but then when you've been a military historian as long as I have, you can't help but admire the fellow. He's got balls, Margaret. And missiles. Okay, so he might be a bit moody, but Christ, who wouldn't be, stuck in Bongo-Bongo land with only nig-nogs for company? But his heart's in the right place. If I were you, Margaret, I'd sack that fat spastic twerp Ken Clarke and put Saddam in the Cabinet. So it might not be popular with the pinko brigade, but what have they ever done for you?"

Her bountiful globes rose with her every breath. "Yes, yes..." she said, distractedly, and motioned away from me with a nod of her head, a sure sign a woman's got the absolute hots and is gasping for it.

I arrived back home rather late that night — and between these four walls I wouldn't be at all surprised if Margaret didn't too! I'm not saying anything happened, but I'm not saying anything didn't happen either! She

obviously loves a true aristocrat, a man of sophistication, class and understated distinction. Cwor! Oy, oy! Way-hay-hay! Wheeee!

Of all the disloyal little creeps, none come more disloyal than my fellow Ministers under Thatcher. What a shower! No sooner had I told everyone what the others had said behind closed doors, than they'd pass it on!

For instance, I once told Michael (Heseltine) that Tom (King) didn't think that Michael (Howard) thought much of the way Leon (Brittan) was going round telling tales on Willie (Whitelaw) for spreading rumours that Cecil (Parkinson) was gossiping about what Kenneth (Baker) had said to David (Young) about there being too much backbiting in the Cabinet — and he immediately went and told Norman (Fowler) who went and told Michael (Heseltine)! But then it's absurd to expect my own high moral standards to be reproduced in a Cabinet full of the most ghastly riff-raff, some of whom have only two houses, if that! No wonder they wouldn't let a man of my proven integrity and position into their oiky Cabinet! Am overcome by a mad urge to piss over the lot of them from a great height. Instead, decide to publish my diaries.

JILLY
COOPER

Men!! But, having said that, I can't help but feel just a mite boo-hoo-ish about poor old Radovan Karadzic. He must be hurting terribly. He looks such a sweetie but so utterly lost, poor love, with that simply *blissful* head of hair blowing this way and that across his poor old furrowed brow as if not quite knowing which way to turn. I know how he feels, because I went through the same sort of thing when Leo ran off with someone else, and deeply gloomy I was too, but that's meant to be jolly private and I literally never mention it, not even now. There I go again!

There's such a lot of unhappiness around at the moment, what with the recession and poor Fergie and Bosnia and that awful spell of rain we had last week and the beastly IRA and our lovely dog Josie having to go to our darling vet for fleas. This means that on top of everything else I simply can't bear to see Radovan looking so very, very miz.

" 'Serbs' him jolly well right!"(!) some will say, but I can't help feeling the big softie could do with a bit of a cuddle, a jolly good night's sleep and a rattling yarn, so let's hope ·

the Red Cross reach Raddie with a copy of my latest book before those tears start plopping on his pillow, poor love,

Rushed off my feet with this book, I've already got going on my next, which is going to be completely different and awfully artistic, set in lovely snowy Norway at the turn of the century, with lots of friendly huskies and really smashing reindeer and super cuddly polar bears.

The plot is going to be very, very Norwegian — "Nor-way" to treat a lady, you might say! — with our hero, Sven Lloyd-Johnson, impossibly handsome, chasing after all the married women in the little Norwegian community of Cosytown-on-Fjord, but eventually falling absolutely madly in love with the lovely heroine, Brigitte, or Brigie for short, who's always a bit of a mess and can't stop bursting into absolute fits of giggles at all the wrong moments but has an insatiable passion for mongrels and a pet moose called "Moose at Ten" (!) and is blessed with an utterly blissful heart of gold.

Of course, there's simply oodles of the most super sex in the book, very passionate and deliciously steamy and very, very Norwegian. In this opening passage, Sven has it off with Hedda, or Heddie, on the tundra he has just had laid — at the most frightful expense — outside his £2,000,000 mansion. Quite a turn-on — or "tundra-on" I think you'll agree!:

"Sven was like the most amazingly bouncy energetic dog when it came to sex. He insisted on eating minced morsels out of a bowl on the floor before leaping onto his latest love.

"When he leapt at last, Heddie, super, adorable, kind-hearted Heddie, who looked rather like the lovely, brilliant Anne Diamond when she became a TV superstar in Britain a full eight years later, lovely Heddie was waiting for him like an obedient

Spaniel, her ears flapping over the sides of the pillows.

"There followed three hours of deliriously passionate love-making, absolutely super and hardly messy at all. For Heddie, it was like nothing she had ever imagined before: like winning all the rosettes at the very best gymkhana and seeing the most fabulous film and being awfully naughty and stealing some chocolate mousse from the fridge and having a jolly good giggle and all at the same time! It was super to be a sexy girl in Norway at the turn of the century, she thought.

"When it was all over, Sven picked up his 19th century Norwegian mobile phone and forcefully tapped out a number with his wildly masculine forefinger. 'Hello!' he barked, setting the scene, 'This is ruthless but irresistible Sven calling from Norway. The time is 1901, just one year into the new century.

"Suddenly, Sven felt the utterly overwhelming urge to make a Norwegian pun. 'Let me inform you that there hasn't been much sunshine here. Also, thank goodness I'm not a soldier outside Buckingham Palace,' he said, a smile lighting up his heart-stoppingly fanciable face, 'or otherwise it wouldn't be so much "the turn of the century" as "the tan of the sentry"!!!' From the other end came simply gales of merriment. No-one in Norway had ever made a joke before, and this was simply the best ever.

I'm sorry, but I really and absolutely don't, don't, DON'T want to say anything about that awful business a couple of years ago when lovely, kind Leo had his little thingy with that poor sweet love of a woman — let's not name her for her own good — who must be hurting dreadfully, poor thing. It was just one of those simply dreadful damp-hankie-ish sobby sorts of things, and I have vowed not to talk about it in public, but to let bygones be bygones, and it would be just so frightfully unfair on her, poor poppet, to rake over it all again in print, going on about all the ghastly unhappiness she caused, poor love, and all the simply horrid hurt she brought onto us all by being so very, very public about it, poor lamb, so I'd like to make it quite clear that in my new book the character of Grizelda Garst-Leigh, the hideous, fat-thighed, semi-alcoholic, fifteentimes married utter tart, poor love, and the character of the internationally successful overweight publisher Leo Olde-Lecher, married to lovely, bubbly, tremendously sexy yet discreet and utterly loyal media superstar Gillie, are all entirely fictitious, and have nothing to do with the true-life characters they're completely based on, poor loves.

Today I felt like strolling out into the country so I went for a lovely long country walk in the tremendously jolly countryside around our country house which is right bang in the middle of the country, completely surrounded on all sides by country, and I was walking towards a country wood — best foot "for-wood"!! — when I thought, "Golly, how lucky I am to live here, right in the middle of the countryside, full of country air and country people and country-ish things to do". But then I thought, "But golly, I love London too, with all my chums and jaunts and giggles and flirts and shops and devastatingly good-looking men and cars and buses and Londony things!" In an ideal world, I thought, London would be in the very centre of the countryside, and the countryside would be in the very centre of London, so then everyone would be happy and we wouldn't have this ghastly recession any more and Fergie would cheer up and Raddie would smile and everyone would begin to realise that Norman Lamont is a lovely, lovely man and a smashing host and they'd stop going at him in that beastly way. Poor love, he's hurting dreadfully. Hey-ho! Time for a drinkie with the lovely kind Leo, poor silly poppet! Men!!

CRIMEWATCH UK

Nick Ross: Imagine, if you will, a leafy suburb with dappled trees, level footpaths and the sun glinting on freshly-installed high-security systems. The kind of place, you might think, where violence was a stranger, where seemingly motiveless crazed knife attacks occur only very rarely.

And that's precisely what reputable estate agent Ian Marks was thinking when he woke up in his own hard-won Wokingham maisonette at 7.30 in the morning ready for another hard day's work:

(Alarm clock rings)

Reputable Estate Agent Ian Marks: Gosh. it's 7.30 in my Wokingham maisonette. Great, Not a single seemingly motiveless crazed knife attack during the night. But then, they do occur only rarely. I must be getting to work now. Bye love. See you tonight without so much as a scratch on my body.

Nick Ross: But that was where he was wrong. By the time the evening had arrived, reputable estate agent Ian Marks had been declared dead, the victim of that very same seemingly motiveless crazed knife attack that he had least expected. To Detective Inspector Bert Snipes of the Berkshire CID,

the crime had all the classic hallmarks of a seemingly motiveless crazed knife attack of the type most of us least expect.

D.I Snipes: Good morning, Sergeant, this body has very many knife wounds in it. In my exp-erience this suggests to me that the victim has been killed by a knife.

Sergeant: Right, Detective Inspector. Do you think the knife was acting alone, or could someone have been holding it?

D.I Snipes: I think you may be onto something, Sergeant. At this stage, we certainly must not rule out the possibility that the knife was not acting alone.

Nick Ross: Detective Inspector, what sort of a man are we looking for here?

D.I Snipes: At a guess, I'd say he was the sort of man capable of carrying out a seemingly motiveless crazed knife attack.

Nick Ross: Any clues to his appearance?

D.L Snipes: Yes, we have some excellent clues. We believe that we could well be on the lookout for a youth or a middle-aged man, maybe someone getting on in years, and that he or she must have had at least one hand with which to perpetrate this vicious crime. We also reckon he or she may have been the kind of person who had access to a knife.

Nick Ross: So, someone with his or her own kitchen, perhaps, or access to someone else's?

D. I Snipes: Correct.

Nick Ross: And I'm told that calls identifying a number of one-or-two-handed men and women somewhere between the ages of 12 and 82 with ready access to kitchens are already coming in, so that's exciting news there. Sue?

Sue Cook: Most of us will, at one time or another, have been gagged, raped and hacked to death. But statistics suggest that this unpleasant combination will occur only once during the lifetime of the average person, so there's no reason to be scared, unless, of course, it's you who's going to be next. So, please, don't worry your little heads.

For professional woman Liz Lockhead the dream of appearing on television was to turn to nightmare when a photograph of her dismembered corpse was featured on the 9 o'clock news last April. This was a particularly brutal murder, in sharp contrast to some of the more gentle and caring murders we have featured in the past. Police are looking for an extremely badly-drawn man with two eyes and what looks a bit like a face. Nick?

Nick Ross: Nasty stuff there, but, please, cheer up: at least the victim wasn't you — not this time at any rate!

We now turn to a particularly gruesome crime, really disgusting, so do please keep watching. It occurred in London's West End, where for centuries ordinary decent Londoners have come to do their shopping and take in a show, going about their business in a perfectly orderly middle-class fashion. But it was just one such ordinary decent shopper who was to find that his trip of a lifetime was to turn into the trip of a deathtime ...

Ordinary decent shopper: Hmmm... this is a lovely fridge-freezer. I am at present considering its purchase.

Masked gunman: Take this, you much-loved family man!

Nick Ross: Seconds later, this much-loved family man was to wake up to find himself dead in a pool of blood. The stains on the carpet ensured that the store itself was left with a ruinously expensive bill running to many tens of pounds — no small amount in a time of recession, making this, as I said, a particularly thoughtless murder. Detective

Constable Jacqui Haines, a man was spotted standing over the body with a sawn-off shotgun — could that be significant?

DC Jacqui Haines: Well, Nick, it —

Nick Ross: Thank you, Detective Constable Jacqui Haines, I'm Nick Ross. We now turn to a particularly savage crime, involving a handheld camera, three men in balaclavas, an old lady lying on the floor in tears, a director desperate to work on *The Bill*, seven out-of-work actors and eight good long chunks of gratuitous violence, Superintendent Hatcher, tell me, when did this particularly unpleasant assault on a senior citizen occur?

Supt. Hatcher: During studio hours, with some outside location work plus full catering facilities.

Nick Ross: I understand that the incident itself has not yet actually occurred, and that this was simply a reconstruction of a crime we would like to see take place with some urgency, now that we have cast it and worked out the necessary camera angles and so forth?

Supt. Hatcher: That is correct, Nick. We would ask anyone wishing to be involved in a fast-moving and dramatic crime such as this to contact us on the incident desk as soon as they have perpetrated it.

Nick Ross: We'll be waiting for your call. And remember — violent crime is much rarer than people tend to think, but we're not going to let that worry us, are we? And whatever happens — don't have nightmares. Do sleep well. Despite the axeman lurking in the spare bedroom.

HUNTER DAVIES

Ooh-er. Crikey It's your old mate Hunter's turn at the diary this week then is it? Blimey O'Reilly, as me old nan used to say. Oh, well. Hold on to your horses, chums. Here we go. Tee hee. Should be a chuckle.

Did you see that Nelson Mandela on telly the other night, did you? Not half bad, that bloke. It doesn't seem long since I interviewed him in prison. So what you in 'ere for, me old mate, I asked him — driving offence, is it?

Turned out he said he was a prisoner of the South African Regine. Looked her up later and what do you know but she's a nightclub owner from Paris, bit overweight for my tastes but not bad for a middle-aged bird. Fancy her locking him up all those years, eh? Bit kinky, or what?

So I said to him stuck there in prison, I said, look Nels, me old lad, haven't you got a bit of a bee in your bonnet about this apartheid wotsit? Just my luck — he started to bang on about freedom and equality. Becoming all philosophical on us, are we, I thought. Not now, Mandy. In my book too many long words is bad for the old indigestion. So I made my excuses. And vamoosed.

But not before I'd caught the flavour of the bloke. First of all, he's black — and why not? Second, he's a legend in his own lifetime, like my old mate Ringo Starr. And third, you can't help but admire him for sticking at it. Can't have been easy, and all that. And, you know what? These insights, what I jotted down in my little red book nearly twenty years ago, these insights still hold true today. Quite a nifty old Hunter, huh?

Insights. That's the name of the game in the interviewing game, I suppose you could say if you had half a mind. That, plus a command of the old mother tongue. English, good and proper. And snappy. What do I try to do when I do what I try to do when I do it then? Good question. Rightio, playmates. I'll try and give you an honesterooni answer. My very bestest interviews give you unexpected insights into the heart of the bloke — or bird! — what I've been interviewing, Sometimes, it means asking the questions no one else asks and catching the toffs and celebs on the hop. Like, when I was interviewing Professor (no less!) Ernst Gombrich in '78, I stopped him halfway through his first arty-farty reply and said: "Ernst — that's a funny name for a bloke! What happened to that second 'e' then — lost it somewhere did you, mate?" And that was when he told me it was the Australian spelling, and that he'd been born a baby on the Australian/Hungarian border "You know something, Ernie — I thought it wasn't English," I said. And he looked positively amazed at my insight. Top marks for Hunter. Clever bugger, Ernst, I'll grant you, but a bit too brainy for the likes of us, eh?

"Pablo — that's a funny name! Anagram or something is it?" I remarked to the world famous painter Pablo Picasso when I met him back in the sixties. Cut the ice, and all that. Set him at his ease. Half the trick in this biz.

Dead nifty with a paint brush, Picasso. But as I said to him at the time, that one's got three eyes and something wonky going on with her neck, Pablo. And when was the last time you saw yellow fingers with green dots!? My own daughter Caitlin could do better than that. With her eyes closed. And she's only five. Might come out more realistic if you took up photography. Amazing what you can do with a Brownie these days, Pablo, providing you get the sun behind you and tell the little lady to say cheese. But would he listen? Would he heckers. Nice one, Pab.

Books? You know the things, lots and lots of pages with lots of little wordies all over them and the author's name in great big swanky letters on the cover? You got it, hole in one. Now you're with me. I'm a bit of a book factory. Can't stop it. Thirty-five bookies behind me at the last count. Literary biogs, mainly. Posh, huh?

What I'm working on now is a biog of Marcel Proust, the dead Frog writer with a moustache, bit like mine. Grrr. The copycat. You've got to have an angle in this game, and my angle is he's far more of an ordinary, decent sort of bloke than the namby-pamby elitist academic types have given him credit for. 'Cos in my opinion he wasn't French at all, he was much more straightforward than that, in my opinion he was born in the North West of England, Carlisle, that sort of area, and just put on a French accent p'raps to pull the birds. But enough of the blab. Judge for yourselves, mates, when it hits your bookstands: "An Eye for the Ladies: A Biography of Marcel Proust" by HUNTER DAVIES should be out come the autumn. One for the Chrissie stocking, eh, chums?

"Don't tell me you wouldn't prefer to be someone like Madonna or Cindy Crawford?" I asked Dame (if you will!) Iris Murdoch the last time I put my head round her tome-lined door, "Not really," she said. Ooooh — fibber! These brainy blue-stocking types really don't understand the half of it when it comes down to brass tacks. Hands up who's read the whole way through an Iris Murdoch? Thought so. There you have it. It's one thing to write one of her books. But it's another thing entirely to sit down and read it. Mind you, she makes a nice cuppa tea, does Iris, so I'm not complaining — and if she gets the Booker Prize and all that pompous claptrap, well, who's complaining? Not me. Honest. My books are for reading on a rainy day by the general public, not just for winning classy prizes. And anyway, Iris Murdoch never wrote the acclaimed authorised biography of The Beatles, now, did she, and she's not personal friends with Paul and she hasn't got a moustache and she's not known as the fifth Beatle, no, is she? So put that in your pipe and puff on it, Iris. Lovely lady, incidentally: very ordinary.

Went to the theatre last night. Very posh do. Classy progs. Plush seats. Curtain up. Yummy lollies in the interval. The lot. Hamlet, it was. Bit wordy. Not much action. Only decent bird goes and gets herself drowned. Set in Denmark. Of all places. So-called hero moons around doing bugger all for three hours. Not a single song you can hum. Yawn, yawn. Can't see it catching on. Much prefer that Meldrew character on the gogglebox. Worra laugh, eh?

A lot of people write. To me. No kidding. And they ask. How can I write. Like you. Blah blah blah. And guess what. My advice is. Don't stint on the full stops. Everyone loves a full stop, Especially if it signals the end of one of my articles. Nice one, Hunt. Must rush. Kissy kissy. Nuff said.

SIR
ROBIN DAY

It is not for the humble television legend — the veteran interviewer, for over thirty five years, of over eight Prime Ministers and countless dozens of Cabinet Ministers — to pull rank on those who seek to follow him. That is something I would never do.

The younger generation of television interviewers — I won't name them for, quite frankly, I can't remember what they're called — need no advice from me, even though my services to our democratic process have been acknowledged, time and time again, by countless awards and chancellorships, by longstanding friendships with many of the leading figures of state and, of course, by my well deserved knighthood in 1981.

But a kindly word, if I may, in the ears of those young whippersnappers who wish to follow in my footsteps. There are interviewers around today who seem to think it awfully clever to be snide, supercilious or downright offensive. It is almost as if they do not feel themselves privileged to be in the company — if only for a few minutes — of some of the greatest politicians of our day. This was never my way. Far from it. When interviewing figures of immense stature on the world stage such as Ted Heath or Jim Callaghan, I could be firm, yes, tough, yes, but never discourteous. Needless to say, some have seen fit to ·criticise me for simply indulging in "Establishment swordplay" or to accuse me of "sucking up" to my interviewees in private. But nothing could be further from the truth, as Ted, Jim and countless other great statesmen are at pains to assure me every time we enjoy a drink and a laugh together.

In 1957, I drew up a six-point code for the ideal television interviewer which I submitted as statutory five-point guidelines to the Director General of the day, whose name now, sadly, escapes me. I still stand by them.

1) The television interviewer must do his duty as a journalist, meeting with his interviewees at private functions and party conferences to exchange compliments on a one-to-one basis.

2) He should wear a bow-tie at all times to distinguish himself from the riff-raff.

3) However distinguished he may be, he should never allow any Prime Minister or World Leader to be unduly awed in his presence.

4) He should always be prepared to make himself available for chat-shows, quiz-games, mid-morning magazine programmes and song-and-dance routines whilst affecting always to despise them.

5) He should remember that a television interviewer is not employed as a debater, prosecutor, inquisitor, psychiatrist or third-degree expert, but as a highly-skilled journalist seeking to impress the full majesty of his intellect on the viewer at home.

6) When offered cigars, meals and after-dinner drinks by leading politicians, he should accept them with good grace, perhaps offering a little tender banter in return.

Incidentally, my younger colleagues can judge for themselves whether their own performances match up to the high standards of this code. I pass on this suggestion without comment, finding it more judicious and dignified to leave it to the persons in question to judge their own pitiful worth.

Many of my television interviews have, I humbly submit, gone down in history as prime examples of the productive cut-and-thrust between world statesmen and highly professional television interviewer. For instance, this exchange with Edward Heath in 1972 has entered the annals as a prime example of the interviewer's art, and I make no apology for reprinting it here:

RD: Mr Heath, Thank you for inviting me here today.

HEATH: I am grateful to you, Robin, for giving me the opportunity to explain our policies to your viewers.

RD: Thank you, Prime Minister.

HEATH: I think it's for me to thank you. Robin.

RD: And why should that be?

HEATH: Why should what be?

RD: Why should it be that it's for you to thank me, Prime Minister?

HEATH: Because, as I have just said, I am grateful to you, Robin, for giving me the opportunity to explain our policies to your viewers.

RD: A lot of people may be surprised at that remark, Prime Minister —

HEATH: They may indeed, Robin! *(laughs)*

RD: But even your opponents would not argue with the proposition that you are no stranger to surprises! Once again, Prime Minister, you have surprised us all.

HEATH: Thank you, Robin.

RD: No — thank *you* Prime Minister.

HEATH: Now, if I could just say one or two words on our statutory incomes policy...

RD: I'm sorry, Mr Heath, but that's all we have time for. Thank you very much.

HEATH: Thank you, Robin.

(MUSIC AND TITLES. CLOSE)

HEATH: Well. you gave me a pretty rough ride there, Robin!

RD: Not too rough, I trust, Ted!

HEATH: Will you stay for a quick drink?

RD: Delighted to, Ted. I must say, I thought we both came over very well, and that's the main thing.

HEATH: Yes, that's the main thing. Sherry, Robin — or something a little stronger?

Why are the young sprigs so rude? The other day, I went along to *Good Morning with Anne and Nick*, a television entertainment of which I had never previously heard, to promote my new book. I was my usual genial self, and they loved me for it.

"So what's the book about, Sir Robin?" says the young man.

"You should have done your homework, boy!" I retort.

"It's your interviews, is it?" says the young woman.

"I'm not hanging around here to be asked impertinent questions like that, young lady."

"I think it's fair to say you're a legend in your own lifetime, Sir Robin." adds the young man.

"How dare you! How downright offensive! What is this show, anyway, and which one are you? Are you the man or the woman?"

Needless to say, everyone seemed delighted by my untiring wit and bonhomie. If only there were more proper gentlemen like me around, one might not fear for the future of British broadcasting. As it is, rampant egotism and rudeness reign.

THE DUKE AND DUCHESS OF DEVONSHIRE

*A*ndrew Devonshire: February is the month I devote to re-arranging the cushions on the sofa in my dressing room, and I do so without any help whatsoever from our staff. As you might imagine, it is quite a job, there being no less than four cushions, each of a different colour. Thus one might choose to arrange the navy blue on one side, the pink on the other, with pale yellow and lincoln green somewhere in the middle, only to find that, on second thoughts, it actually looks better to have the pink somewhere in the middle, with the pale yellow to the left, the navy blue to the right, leaving room for the lincoln green to remain in the middle, only this time next to the pink and not to the pale yellow, unless of course it is between the pink and the pale yellow. Whenever I have met them, I have found that the British public are extraordinarily ignorant of the demands and pressures with which we in the so-called "upper classes" are confronted day by day. I sometimes think that the "ordinary" people, for all their immense pluck, fail to appreciate the many onerous tasks that befall the Stately Home owner, and I welcome this opportunity to "put them in the picture". Re-arranging the cushions on the sofa in my dressing-room is one such

task, and the time and planning involved are not to be underestimated. First, I have one of our staff nip out to the local shops to buy me a range of excellent new French devices known as "crayons", which are what we used to know as pencils, but with brightly coloured leads. I then spend a week or so measuring out on a piece of paper and colouring in four squares — pink, pale yellow, lincoln green and navy blue — and a further week cutting them out. This leaves me just a fortnight to juggle these four coloured squares around this way and that, until I am perfectly satisfied that I have "come up" with the best new arrangement. It all makes for a highly enjoyable topic of dinner conversation too, and, come February, our guests delight in spending an hour and a half or so over the soup arguing the pros-and-cons of, say, having the pink on the left or the pale yellow on the right, and thoroughly productive it is too.

*D*eborah Devonshire: The second week of February is now virtually over, and I still haven't found time to assist poor Andrew with the uphill struggle he is having with the rearrangement of his cushions, so utterly hectic has my own life been, what with the frightful bother of trying to impose some semblance of order on my scarf drawer. "Scarf" — that's an interesting word, and of course "cushion" is another, and we discussed how interesting they were over dinner the night before last. Norman St John of Fawnsley pointed out that there is no other word in the English language spelt c-u-s-h-i-o-n, in that order, and when I pointed out that it is also the only word in English spelt exactly in that way meaning something you can sit on, darling Roy Strong got tremendously over-excited, clapping his hands together, and was kind enough to tell me how clever I was!! The two of them were such utter poppets that after they had finished their main courses I told them they could get off their knees for pudding and sit with us around the grown-ups table. (Memo to self: "table" — now that's an interesting word, and worthy of fuller discussion among my houseguests over the course of March.)

Andrew Devonshire: Has anyone solved the problem of what to do when you reach the end of the right-hand page when reading a book? It really is an awful chore to attempt to what I believe is now known as "turn the page over". Often the pages turn two, or even three, at a time, so that one loses one's place and misses some major event that may or may not have happened in those two or three pages, and, even if one does manage to turn just the one page, one still encounters the problem of having to re-organise one's fingers and hands so as to incorporate the freshly-turned page. Of course, during the daytime, one can call for a highly-skilled member of one's staff to perform the necessary feat — and they do so with great dexterity, I might add — but while reading in bed at night, for instance, it really is too tiresome to have to ring one's bell so that some poor fellow has to come running in his nightshirt. One solution, of course, if the book consists of 200-odd pages, is to buy 200-odd copies of the book, and to ask the bookseller politely if he will pre-open each book to a fresh page, but I imagine this solution may present some storage disadvantages for those living in the more modest stately homes, "bungalows", and so forth. Incidentally, I am at present reading, and greatly enjoying, a book called "Rearranging Your Upstairs Cushions", available through the National Trust, as I may or may not have told you that February is the month I devote to re-arranging the cushions on the sofa in my dressing room — quite a chore as it turns out!!

Deborah Devonshire: I was intrigued to learn recently that there is now a product on the market which can turn bread into "toast", without any need for all the palaver of toasting fork, fire, butler and so forth. This splendidly ingenious contraption is called a "toaster", comes in a variety of colours and can be obtained from many leading shops. What on earth will they think of next? Andrew and I now spend many a happy hour making toast, by simply placing a slice of bread (which now comes "ready-sliced", would you believe?) into the slot in the "toaster", pressing the button down, and waiting a minute or two before it "pops up". If one wants a second slice, one simply buys another toaster and repeats exactly the same moves again. Buttering the toast is another matter, which we feel safest leaving to our excellent cook. Isn't it about time someone invented a contraption so that buttering, too, became the proverbial "piece of cake"? How well I remember in the old days my sisters Dipso and Bimbo and Commie and Loopi and I all having an absolute whale of a time attempting to butter a piece of bread by holding the bread in our hands and passing it roughly over the wodge of butter, but we met with little success, so — with typically delightful aristocratic eccentricity! — we simply threw the butter out of an upstairs window for all the simply marvellous little servants to enjoy! I wonder what happened to that concept of fun, or is it now considered "old-fashioned" or — worse! — "square" ...?

Andrew Devonshire: The month of March — one of my favourites — is just round the corner, and another chore looms, for March is always the month I devote to plumping up the cushions I will have just re-arranged on the sofa in my dressing room. But which should I plump up first — the pink or the pale yellow or the lincoln green or the navy blue? At the beginning of the month, we will be throwing a Ball for some of our greatest friends in order to discuss the matter. Desperately hard work, yes, exhausting, yes, but such are the obligations and duties that come with the ownership of one of our great historic houses.

CHRIS EVANS

It's me, yes, no, yes — yes, it's me, Chris Evans, Monsieur Christopherrrrrrrrr Evans, saying we've got a lot coming up in the next few paragraphs so stay reading, whatever you do stay reading. Bloke came up to me in a swanky club last night and said, "Hey, you Chris Evans?" What a nutter, eh? What-a-nutter! So I said, "Well, Thick Bloke, name one other person I could be?!" — that shut him up, I can tell you! You Chris Evans indeed. Who else? You gotta laugh. Anyway, as I was saying, coming up soon we've got the real story behind what I was saying to myself before the show began and an update on what was happening in yesterday's show and later we've got our On The Bog slot and before that we've got Honk Your Horn and then in an actiononolio-packed show we've also got the regular Pissed My Pants item and of course our regular farting competition, yes it's our very own Blow Off Down The Blower. What a programme, it's so huge it'll make the girls gasp, and then they'll all be gagging for it eh? Hey! Stand back boys!

So like I said, coming up in the next few paragraphs we've got Honk Your Horn, we've got On The Bog, we've got Pissed My Pants and Blow Off Down The Blower and we've also got — yeah!!!! oooh-wooh! — we've also got the splendigorgeous Tina with the Traffic — wooh! How would you like to take my Two-Tonner up your service area, eh, Tina?! Hahahaha!

Tina: Hahahahahahah reeely brilyernt Chris!

News is just coming in of a major traffic pile-up involving an overturned lorry on the clockwise section of the M25 between junctions 8 and 9! Brilyernt!

I'd "pile up" on you any day in my overturned lorry, Tina! Hahahaha! Any tragic deaths, love?

Tina: Just a couple, I'm afraid, Chris.

Ah well, better than none at all, Tina — and I wouldn't mind "coupling" with you tonight either!!! Hahahaha, brilliant traffic news plus two tragic deaths from Tina there and coming up we've got music from Splurge, Toxic Poison, Adenoid, Squirm and Brain Dead plus the totally new single from Acne Triumphant plus all your fave regular slots like Slit Your Wrists Off where today's listener cuts his or her foot off and wins a brand new — woooh! — a spanking new I Slit My Wrists For Chris Evans exclusive Radio 1 T-Shirt, can't be bad, and also coming up soon is the Coming Up Soon slot, where I let you know what's coming up in the next few minutes. What or who are you looking most forward to Coming Up, Tina? On second thoughts, don't answer that! Hahahaha!

Phew! What a weird weekend that was! Weeeeeird! I mean, I met so many PEOPLE! Like, one two three four five six seven eight nine people, actually more like thirty or forty entirely new PEOPLE! And I'd like to say hello to everyone we met this weekend. I can't mention them all individually but I'd just like to say hello to them all, whoever they were, and they weren't anyone much, or else I'd be mentioning them individually, you can be sure of that! Hahahaha! And now it's Fact of the Day time again at four minutes to eight, and today's surprising fact is that It's Official — It's Unsafe to Eat Poisonous Snakes: doctors in Colorado have confirmed that it's unsafe to eat poisonous snakes — blimey! bet it is, I can't see myself tucking into a poisonous snake — I'm more a fish and chips with a few beers man meself! Tina

— how'd you like to see my poisonous snake, love? Tongue out or in? Hahahaha! So to everyone I met at the weekend, we've got the latest from MC and the DMCs featuring X Ray and DSMs — and by the way, has that Liz Hurley got big bazookas or what? Only kidding, Liz! Over to Tina for the news right out UPFRONT at seventeen minutes past eight. Hahahaha, Tina?

Tina: And the biggest news today is that Take That have scheduled their new album for October, PLUS three hundred people have been killed in the latest outbreak of tragic atrocities in the Bosnia region of the world and former James Bond man Roger Moore is set to make his screen comeback — only this time as a villain — all the details on these and other BIIIG stories coming up soon. Chris!!?

Thanks, Teens. Now we've got Sue from Bridport on the phone, hi Sue, how y'doin?

Fine.

And where you from, Sue from Bridport?

Bridport!

Yeah! Wooh! And you're what? An ordinary housewife!

That's right Chris — an ordinary housewife!

And where did you say you were from, Sue?

From Bridport, Chris.

And your name is?

Sue.

And what did you say you did, Sue?

I'm an ordinary housewife, Chris.

Well, thanks Sue from Bridport — lovely talkin' to you, Sue — and you can suck my cock any day!!! And coming up soon, a major accident on the M6 and after I've finished talking the last thirty seconds or so of the latest huge single from Glum — all this, after this.

Shall I shut up? It'd be nice, wouldn't it, eh? Have I told you I'm happy? I haven't? Well, I am. Do you prefer oranges or lemons? Let us know — coming up soon, the number to ring. And what about that Liz Hurley? Woooh! And as I've said the Fact of the Day is now what was it? Oh well, if you know

the capital of Singapore — like Michael Hutchence, he's a Singer Poor, gerrit? then let us know, but the big question — it's really GINORMOUS, Tina, promise, gerremoff — is should I shut up? It'd be nice, wouldn't it, eh? But I can't, I can't, I can't — or else what would become of our move to take Radio 1 right upmarket — you can go up my market any time, Liz Hurley! — and to target a brand new kind of super-intelligentibobbles rock listener? Coming up soon, Blow Off Down The Blower, and I'll be giving you all the news of what I was up to last night, plus all the latest from the hunkiest motorway disasters around the country and the new single from Loathsome Shower. Are we having fun, or what?

These We Have Loved

LORD GOODMAN

Over the years, the Queen has sought my advice on many matters of a distressing nature, none of which I am prepared to divulge here. I always find her warmly appreciative. Recently She has, between ourselves, most considerately expressed Her personal thanks for my role in the removal of the Berlin Wall, and earlier this year she warmly congratulated me on Robert Stephens' magnificent portrayal of King Lear at Stratford. She was also grateful, I am reliably informed, for my part in seeing that Mr Neil Armstrong arrived safely on the surface of the moon, and She likewise admired the way I brought about through a mixture of good sense and patience a united Europe. Of my major backstage role in more recent events — the engagement of Viscount Linley to Miss Serena Stanhope, the completion of the Channel Tunnel, the upturn in the fortunes of the England Cricket XI, a swift conclusion to the conflict in the Gulf, the reduction in our trade deficit — She is silently supportive, as indeed She would be well advised to be, if She values Her reputation.

MARIANNE FAITHFULL

Give me a break. It really pisses me off. After the drugs bust and all the publicity surrounding it, I was stuck for years with this ridiculous rock-star-moll image, invented by the gutter press and the cops and the establishment purely to discredit me and my generation and all the changes we wanted in society.

"You know something, Keith, it really pisses me off, this rock-star-moll image I've been saddled with," I said to Keith when we were lying in bed one day.

"Yeah," he replied, sympathetically, and then he said: "Hang on, it's quarter past. It's Mick's turn."

Mick was great. Lying in bed with him seemed to put things in perspective. "You know something, Mick," I said. "It really pisses me off, this rock-star-moll image I've been saddled with. And the Establishment's always trying to make out that we're all on drugs."

"Don't blaggard the spliff, babe," said Mick. Then a look of agitation came over his face. "Hang on," he said. "There's something bumpy at the bottom of the bed — go an' see what it is, babe, be a doll."

So I gave Mick the spliff and made my way through the sheets to the bottom of the bed. On the way down, who should I meet but Brian Jones with his familiar hangdog expression. "What you doing here, Brian?" I said.

"I'm forming an orderly queue, Marianne", he replied. It was then that I noticed a couple of Small Faces, a Trogg and three or four Swinging Blue Jeans behind him, plus their roadie. carrying a catering pack of Mars Bars.

"Hands up which of you has read Rimbaud recently?" I said. This was the way things happened in the Sixties. You'd talk about what books you'd read and if you found you were on the same astral plain you'd go to bed together.

The whole lot of them put their hands up. "So what did Rimbaud write then?" I asked the Swinging Blue Jeans.

There was a silence, then their drummer said: "Tintin in Tibet, wasn't it?"

At this point, I could sense that at the top of the bed Mick was beginning to get restless. "What's happenin' down there, Marianne?" he said.

"Nothing, Mick," I replied. Mick could get obsessively jealous, and I didn't want anyone to come between us, even the Swinging Blue Jeans. But when I made my way back to the top of the bed. I caught him snogging with Anita, and sorting things out with his accountants. But this was the Sixties, and in those heady days, everyone snogged with Anita and sorted things out with their accountant, so it was all I cool.

Keith was gorgeous in those days. Totally gorgeous. For years, he was the epitome of my idea of the Byronic soul, so beautiful and pure. I suppose I first realised how beautiful he was when I first saw him opening a tin of Baked Beans using just his tongue. But I hardly ever saw him put any food in his mouth. When the tin was open, he'd put the baked beans, one by one, up his nose. "That way I don't need to clean my teeth more than once a year," he explained. The accumulation of food in his nose probably gave Keith his famous moody, tortured look. Once we had Keith, Brian and Anita over to drop acid and we all sat round the ceiling in our furs, satins and velvets and talked about the fantastic things we would do with the kingdom if only we could, and how we would run the world. Actually, I say we sat round the ceiling, but five hours later and after a lot of thought it turned out to be the floor.

Brian was very much the philosopher of the group, an avid reader who'd read almost all the first chapter of Lord of the Rings. As a result, he'd thought very, very deeply about a whole lot of things. "You can't hold a lot of water in an egg-cup," he announced, and we all thought and thought for a long time and nodded our heads. "I mean, the only water you can hold in an egg-cup is, well, about the size of an egg-cup I suppose. Certainly not bigger, or not much." "Right, right," we all said together.

"If you want to go to the moon, you'll never find it at the bottom of the ocean 'cos the moon is in the sky… " he continued, an hour and a half later. "Never eat a hedgehog if your mouth is made out of balloon… A dead cat will never bark… Green is not yellow but orange is almost yellow, especially if you paint it all over with yellow paint."

Slowly but surely, we were working out a whole philosophy for the way our generation would run the planet. Mick even developed a five point plan of government. "Like, first," said Mick, "I'd clean up your downstairs toilet, Brian." Mick was always very fastidious. "Like, I mean, what's that dead chicken doin' in there for starters? If I was King or President or whatever, I'd say no one's allowed to keep dead chickens in

their lavvies without my written permission, right?"

And so we would go on, setting the world to rights until the early hours of the morning. At about 3am, Mick would say, "Right, let's really start to do something about the world, then" and we'd all try and get to our feet, but we'd just wobble over and lie on our backs, or fall head first into a bean-bag, so we never really got round to it, which really pissed us all off, like it was an establishment conspiracy to keep us away from doing all that good.

There was a constant parade of visitors to the house in Chester Square so we bought another house in Cheyne Walk, and when that began to fill up we moved to Eaton Square. So we had three houses, all full of heads and freaks, but Mick hated untidiness, so he said we had to move anyone who wasn't still breathing out of the upstairs bathroom and into the basement. At this time, I was secretly involved with Spanish Tony who didn't realise I was also intimately attached to Japanese Frank, who had no idea I was having a passionate affair with Nicol Williamson, from whom I kept my on-off relationship with Arthur Askey a firm secret, as I was worried that if he found out he would tell Moroccan Herbert, who was intensely jealous of Freddie and the Dreamers, with whom I was beginning to grow heavily involved, and I was at all costs determined to preserve my dignity.

Once, I'd smoked so much hash that I was feeling a bit catatonic and I suddenly had this nightmare vision of us all thirty years on, still doing exactly the same things, freaking out and jamming and schlepping and getting our rocks off but now, like, *old*, with the Stones still touring and me still feeling really out of it, and the whole Sixties thing still dragging on, and us all selling our stories to the *Daily Mail* in return for dough, regardless of our reputations. I mean, thank god it was only a nightmare, you know?

THE FOOD AND DRINK GANG

Chris Bouffy: 'Tis — as the old adage has it! — the season to be merry — and, on a more serious note, what better way to kick off this festive diary with the very latest in food scares, fresh in today...

There is increasing concern being voiced throughout the entire food-producing community that the ongoing popularity of the traditional Christmas lunch has given rise to a dramatic increase in the death of the turkey population as a whole. In a survey, over 90% of householders questioned who were planning to eat a turkey on Christmas day admitted that their bird would be dead before it reached the table.

These revelations have already triggered widespread concern among the turkey population as a whole, and many leading experts are calling for a complete government crackdown on the outdated practice of eating dead turkeys. To help you serve a live turkey this Christmas, we have produced this BBC Food and Drink leaflet "Best Served Still Clucking". It also shows you how you can have a great deal of fun trying to carve the bird while it runs around your kitchen. But please do be careful when you stuff it — live turkeys have been known to scratch and even bite. And here's our very own Jilly Silly to tell us what to have with it: Jilly — ?

Jilly Silly: Oz and I have had simply LOADS of fun choosing your Yuletide tipple this year. What do I want in my mouth this Christmas? I want something soft, I want something mouthfilling, I want something big and preferably red, I want something I can swirl around my tongue, suck and spit, out I want something huge and simply splendid, something I can really chew on.

Oz Cluck: But to go back to the booze why not try something that little bit different with your meal this year? For instance, I've tried following the marvellous old Indian tradition, made famous by Gandhi —

Jilly Silly: No relation of Goosey Goosey, ha ha!

Oz Cluck: Thanks, Jilly. I've followed this marvellous old Indian tradition of drinking one's own urine. Mmmmm! It smells of new mown hay, it smells of barley-sugar, it smells of last night's curry, it smells of chewing-gum found on the sole of one's right foot after a long walk in a shopping precinct, it smells of anchovy, it smells of kidneys, it smells of a forest vole squashed under the wheel of an oncoming vehicle. Mmmm! And its taste is everything one wants from a urine sample — there's cloves, there's a hint of chocolate, there's lemon, there's ivy, there's apple, there's dandelions, and above everything else there's that marvellous, musky taste one gets from the bottom of one's dustbin after the rain's got into last week's oven scrapings. Chris — ?

Chris Bouffy: Thanks, Oz. Over the past week, a number of viewers have rung in complaining of a large, dark, hairy, oily object that sticks to the outside of frying pans and dribbles. Don't worry, this is just Michael Beardie, our resident chef. Beardie — ?

Michael Beardie: Thanks, Bouffy. Later on, I'll be showing you how you can get very, very fat by eating lots of food very quickly, but now a couple of thoughts on choosing a kitchen table — first, you should choose a table, and second, you should put it in your kitchen. But now how to get very, very fat. It's really very simple. You'll need:

5lbs butter

6lbs duck or goose fat

7lbs clotted cream

8lbs milk chocolate

9lbs doughnuts

10lbs fatty meat

And here's how:

Eat them all up in one go — though for added flavour, if you have the time you might like to try mixing them all together in a large container first. And here — for those watching their weight! — is the Healthy Option.

Exactly the same as above, but add one level teaspoon of fromage frais.

Happy eating!

Chris Bouffy: Sounds delicious. Thanks, Beardie, Amen to that. And now to the dramatic findings of this week's survey, which are already beginning to cause shockwaves of profound indifference throughout the entire British food industry. Senior government nutritionists have discovered that though a packet bought in your High Street supermarket might carry such slogans as "delicious", "tasty" or "full of goodness", these words do not — I repeat NOT — refer to the packet itself, but to the food inside it.

Yet a number of ordinary shoppers continue to be gravely misled. 54-year-old Miss Doreen Daft collapsed on Friday having just eaten a packet marked "Delicious Curry for Two".

"Obviously, I threw away the food inside and tucked into the packet," she said yesterday, "and I am still recovering. I think it's an absolute disgrace that manufacturers can mislead the consumer in this way." And last night, a 63-year-old man, Mr Charles Cretin, was on a life-support machine having eaten a tin of baked beans marked "Mmmm so tasty", after first throwing away the beans inside.

How many more lives will be put at risk before manufacturers clearly mark their packets "DO NOT EAT"? This is an issue which must concern us all. Jilly — ?

Jilly Silly: Mmmmm! This is a real joyful festive absolutely super sparkling lovely happy-making humdinger bouncing bean of a very average table wine! In this wine, there's cinnamon, there's breakfast cereal, probably Special K, there's motor oil, maybe Castrol GTX, there's Grip-Fix, there's a jam doughnut, there's a hint of after-shave, there's a couple of paperback books, there's someone else's lipstick, there's shepherd's pie, there's squid, there's fly spray, there's a couple of glasses of Lucozade, there's a pork sausage and there's a sea anemone. The only trouble is, they've left out the wine. Beardie — ?

Michael Beardie: I'm transfixed by your really super dress, Jilly! On a lighter note, a lot of you have written in to ask me for a handy tip on how to dispose of unwanted leftovers during the festive season. A Mr Yentob from West London writes in to suggest — why not truss them up and place them behind a magimix on their very own BBC2 Christmas show? Great idea, Alan! Chris — ?

Chris Bouffy: On a more serious note, a recent survey suggests that the number of food scares now being issued by the BBC is in danger of rising to unmanageable proportions, threatening the well-being and sanity of every man, woman and child in the country. And do please try to remember not to drink too much deadly poison over the festive season — in some isolated instances it has been known to kill. Happy worrying!

DAVID HARE

The State of Britain, Part One: Three days ago, I went to a party. I don't often go to parties, because I'm not that kind of person, I'm a playwright, with more serious concerns. But I went to this one. By bus, of course. I'm not the sort of person who takes taxis. So I hailed a double-decker in the King's Road and told the driver to take me to Islington. He was then to wait for me outside the party for an hour or two and take me back. The instructions were quite clear. But of course this is Thatcher's Britain, so when I left the party — a party I didn't particularly enjoy, by the way, it was hardly serious at all and full of "amusing" people — the bus was nowhere to be seen (typical) and I was forced to hail, against all my instincts, a black cab. Out of sympathy with the driver I sat with him in the front, observing, observing, observing, my mind racing back to one of those rare defining moments, disproportionately significant but peculiarly illuminating, that had occurred back at the party.

I had been standing in the corner of the room with the dirty paper cup I had specially brought with me, when a man had come over — a tall, flashy type, with an easy smile. wearing a fashionable "tie". He said: "You look a bit lonely, may I introduce myself?" He then introduced himself. I didn't reply,

preferring to observe, as most serious playwrights do. He then said — again that fake smile — "And who are you?"

I was outraged, utterly outraged. And flabbergasted. Shocked too. Shocked, outraged and flabbergasted. Not for me, of course, but for my profession, and the whole of British Theatre, from the lowest understudy right up to the most brilliant and dangerous playwright (whether this is me or not is beside the point). Why was this man — this man in his fashionable tie, with his promiscuous smile and his over-attentive handshake — pretending not to know who the hell I was? This was a sign of our inexorable national decline, as significant and painful in its way as the Miners Strike or the Falklands Conflict.

The State of Britain, Part Two: As the hurt and the horror surged within me, I felt driven to speak. "I'm David Hare," I said.

"David Hare!" he repeated, "Goodness! I really enjoy all your plays — you're one of the greatest living playwrights, in my opinion!"

Note that patronising, biassed and artfully demeaning tone in a statement riddled with the foul odour of ruling class condescension: "*ONE OF* the greatest *LIVING* playwrights, *IN MY OPINION*".

Only in Britain — tired, sick, dislocated, dying Britain — in the 1990s could it be considered "fashionable" to denigrate a serious playwright in this way. When I got home, I immediately wrote a cool letter to the host of the party, questioning his ethics in inviting me to a function at which there were people who openly hated me, roundly condemning his loathsome hypocrisy in not warning me of his treachery. He eventually replied with some sort of an apology. Which all goes to show that here in Thatcher's Britain, the national pastime — the national characteristic — is to apologise, apologise, apologise. When will we as a nation have the courage to start to stand up for ourselves?

The State of Britain, Part Three: I've tried to bring out something of this and other symptoms of our national decline in my new play *Cardboard Characters* — the first part of my powerful new *Forty Winks* trilogy consisting of *Cardboard Characters, Dialogue Dreary* and *An Absence of Interest* — which is currently being staged at The National Theatre. *An Absence of Interest* seeks to analyse the system whereby the ruling classes use the money gained from the working classes to finance other members of the ruling classes to write a trilogy about how they take money from the working classes to finance their systems, a trilogy which will be visited, I hope, not only by other members of the ruling classes but by a few representatives of the working class as well. It is a tremendously strong piece, devastating in its indictment of the inherent hypocrisy of those involved in its creation.

The State of Britain, Part Four: In this truly moving piece of dialogue, the main character is a brilliant yet sensitive playwright, who some people say is based on me but is obviously NOT me at all — I'm not Welsh. In this truly moving piece of dialogue the playwright character, who is called Daffyd Hare, confronts what he sees

as the malaise in the post-colonial Britain:

JACK: Cigarette?

DAFFYD: No thanks.

JACK: You don't want a cigarette

DAFFYD: Not at the moment. No thanks.

JACK: Don't smoke?

DAFFYD: Only when I stop to think about the malaise in post-colonial Britain which stems, directly or indirectly, from our national sense of dislocation, springing, whether consciously or not, from our deeply rooted inability to shed the sense of past glories, a failure which may or may not be rooted in our concurrent inability to face up to the challenges of the future, to develop and expand those institutions that are crumbling around us, unloved and unwanted, fostering an abandoned generation without pride or sense of purpose. *(He frowns. Something is on his mind)*

JACK: Yeah, I keep meaning to give up, too. I did once, for a couple of months, but then I went back. Mug's game, really.

DAFFYD: You're right there, Jack.

JACK: It's not as though I even like the taste, much. How about you?

DAFFYD: I'd relish the taste more if it didn't make me remember the days when hope beat in our hearts, when it seemed as if this country was marching forward into a new age, an age of optimism, an age in which society would look after those who were unable, for whatever reason, to —

JACK *(Looking at watch)*: Lordy be, Daffyd — is that the time? I must be going. Cheerio, then. Lovely talking to you.

DAFFYD *(Frowns)*: I've always wanted to know the answer. The answer to one question. A question that has haunted me. And the question is. After two and a half hours, is this all it's been about. Is it? Well, is it?

(The lights fade)

Well — is it?

(The sound of "Land of Hope and Glory" grows louder. Curtain)

SIR NICHOLAS HENDERSON GCMG

January 19th 1969: Gordon Hordern-Bordern comes into my office to tell me of a crisis in Korea. I get my men on to it, and they come back two hours later, elated. It emerges that Korea is in the Far East. I listen to Gordon patiently, as any modern Ambassador should, but without anxiety. I have heard the full range of Far East problems many times before. I put him at ease by telling him that one of the advantages of the East is that it is indeed so far. When his chuckles have died down, I add that its problems are inherently unsuited to solution, and are likely to continue very messy. He roars with laughter. I top him up with an amusing Ducru Beychevelle and we spend the rest of the day choosing a suitable wedding present for the Eric Honeckers' daughter, and selecting the right smoked salmon for a buffet reception for the Ceaucescus, who are always so very appreciative.

September 3rd 1972: At the risk of spoiling the sport of those who like tilting at windmills, I cannot help thinking that the argument that the function of the diplomat has decreased and continues to decrease rests on a false premise. There is much that we do to blow the trumpet for British Exports. Only yesterday we threw a dinner party in the Bonn Embassy for the one product with which the British continue to lead the world. For the British Driving Glove Manufacturers Annual Dinner, we asked all our foreign dignitaries to wear the British driving gloves provided to the right of their knives. Wearing these highly flexible and marvellously lightweight (23% cotton mix) gloves, they happily tucked into a decent three-course meal with a complimentary glass of wine. Afterwards, they were kind enough to say that these British gloves had offered little or no impediment to their pleasure. In my closing speech, I thanked them all for coming, and reminded them not to remove their driving gloves from the premises, but to return them in orderly fashion to the doorman on their way out. Such dynamic sales-drives are now a vital part of any British Ambassador's life, and are not lightly to be dismissed.

May 24th 1973: After an excellent dinner for the Phatt-Leeches and their 40 guests — Seafood Consommé, Lobster, Cheese, Crème Brûlée, with an excellent Pouilly Fumé — the conversation turns to news from home. It is irredeemably bad: economic decline, rising unemployment, inflation, rising discontent, and goodness knows what else. As the brandy and mints are taken around by the staff, complaints continue to crop up about our "something-for-nothing" society, with its roots in British indolence and greed. By this time, we have all taken the weight off our feet in order to enjoy some first-rate brandy-snaps with our liqueurs. "Can nothing really be done to halt the decline of this once great country of ours?" asks an immensely distinguished visiting statesman. It is generally agreed that only a renewed sense of vigour and national pride could spur our pitiful old country out of its present torpor. But by this time we are all feeling sleepy so, after another brandy or two, we make our separate ways to bed.

December 4th 1977: The arrival of the Prince of Wales has delighted everybody here in our Paris Embassy. He is quite brilliant at shaking hands with everyone, and walks with a natural ease by moving one leg in front of the other. The French adore him, of course, and since his arrival British exports have boomed, with two pairs of British driving gloves sold in the Lyons area alone. After his official duties are over, HRH lets his hair down, retiring to our drawing room to delight us with his imitations, which he performs quite brilliantly. "Have I done my Neddy Seagoon?" he says at 2.00 am. "No sir — that would be lovely," I reply, and he does his Neddy Seagoon for the fifteenth time, while we all applaud wholeheartedly. The role of today's diplomat, working at the coal-face of modern life, is not to be underestimated, even in this day and age of "highspeed technology" — electric toasters and so forth.

March 20th 1978: Gordon Hordern-Bordern comes in to the office to tell me of some sort of crisis in Libya. I listen patiently but without much sense of anxiety as he fills me in on their plans to bomb Western Europe to smithereens. "Why not see if little Gaddafy feels like a spot of lunch, early June or thereabouts? I have an idea he went to Harrow." I suggest. Gordon returns with the news that lunch with Gaddafy in June is out of the question. "No doubt he's an adherent of the ghastly American practice of 'the working breakfast'!" I suggest in a voice not untinged with irony. Gordon tells me Gaddafy is already busy dropping bombs. "Perhaps we should bring lunch forward to May, then," I say, "We could see if the Douarier Duchesse de Mouchy, the Elie de Rothschilds and Odette Pol-Roger might be around to amuse him." Gordon informs me that there is a bomb falling on the Embassy while we speak. "Oh, Lord," I sigh, looking at my watch, "I suppose that means we'd better make room for elevenses with Gaddafy today — any chance of getting some jam doughnuts in and perhaps a dab or two of clotted cream? And I don't suppose Princess Margaret's available? That should do the trick."

December 30th 1981: I have sent my detailed analysis of the Falklands conflict to London. It covers two full pages of foolscap, with hardly a single crossing-out. My summing-up concludes that it consisted of a difference of opinion between two major nations, i.e. Britain and Argentina, and that, by and large, Britain emerged victorious. I also include a summing-up of President Galtieri. I say that he is a military man who rose to the presidency, very Argentinean indeed, with a limited sense of humour. London is delighted with my report. And some people still maintain that the job of an Ambassador is all tea and buns, which are actually in very short supply, owing to Embassy cutbacks.

January 19th 1989: The Prime Minister of Korea is an exceptionally cultured man, a brilliant and congenial scholar and devoted public servant. We were indeed honoured to be able to entertain him to a finger buffet of a selection of finest cuts of British Spam at our Embassy, which has now been moved from the old mansion house to the more convenient and easy-to-clean hut just six miles further along the same road. He assured us that he found our new bring-a-bottle policy highly sensible, and was obviously delighted to meet Major Ronald Ferguson, who had agreed to come along to lend the necessary glamour to the event. The trade agreement went through very smoothly, with Korea agreeing to export millions of pounds of their manufactured goods to us and we, in our turn, agreeing not to send any more of our awful stuff to them. Handshakes all round, leaving just enough time to prepare for a jolly good dinner.

HAPPY CHRISTMAS WITH SUZANNE MOORE

Like hell it is. Is it really appropriate within this culture of ours in which rabid commercialism is disseminating its entrails into every last corner of our so-called lives that we should still refer to the season or seasons of Christmas as "happy"? I wasn't born yesterday, love.

Whichever way you look at it, and believe me I have, Christmas is a male-dominated, male-invented, male-order institution designed to reassert the power and prestige of those in our society with dangly bits between their legs and that doesn't mean me or us. No one can deny that if you take the second letter and the fourth letter and the fifth letter out of cHrIStmas you get the word HIS, so surely I can't be the only one to feel offended by it or is that asking too much of a culture reeling under the impact of fifteen years of the Conservative jackboot? Hardly.

I could do with a bit of gold, and I suppose I could just about manage some frankincense. But Myrrh? Not myrrh-y likely, mate. I wouldn't want a bucketful of myrrh if you left it on my doorstep and paid me five hundred quid to take it off your hands. Myrrh? Myeugh, more like.

Happy? Try telling that to the turkey that's just been trussed and stuffed and placed in the oven at a low temperature for ten gruelling hours. Try telling that to the brussels sprout that until yesterday was hanging on its tree without a care in the world but is now being skinned and slashed and placed in boiling water, leaving her family without any form of a matriarchal brussels sprout as a role-model. The fact of the matter is that there's nothing more upsetting than giving or receiving presents. As Jacques Quacque points out in his seminal work, *The Myth of Human Joy* (1987), the giving of a present is a classic way by which supremacy can be and is and continues to be asserted in our materialistic society, and that's my point. And the whole point about my point is that the point I am making has a larger point, which is that the point of unwrapping a present is the same in the mind of your average man as undressing a woman and must thus be wholly discouraged. And another thing. The last time I was given a "present" (and inevitably, guess who was left to unwrap the damn thing? Right first time: moi) it turned out to be something I didn't want. Typical, and yet another example of the crass "You-scratch-my-back-but-I'll-be-damned-if-I'll-scratch-yours" society we have created for ourselves. No wonder the National Health Service is in decline, and millions of innocent women are starving in Ethiopia. So much for the "triumph" (note the inverted commas) of Goose Green. Still happy, then?

Could someone please tell me pretty damn urgently, why should the holly bear the throne? What's the holly done to deserve it? Paid the odd tenner into the Tory party's secret coffers, no doubt. Arise, Lord Holly, and all that. Meanwhile, the poor bloody ivy — having slogged her damn guts out to get into that carol in the first place — is just simply forgotten by the third verse, banished and neglected so that Holly can reap the dividends of brutal triumphalism. Some Christmas that proved to be for Ivy, eh?

So, it's official. Christmas is once again to be on December 25th. The obscenity of this fact is that last year it was on December 25th, and the year before that, and the year before that, and it's been on December 25th for as long as most of us can remember. It gets on my wick. But did anyone ask us when we wanted it to be? Like as heck they did. Yet when have you ever seen it questioned? Right first time; never. There are more ways to gag someone than putting a gag around their mouth. You can use a hankie, for one. But more puzzling to me than trying to get inside the sick minds of those who place Christmas on exactly the same day every single bloody year and what frankly really scares the hell out of me is trying to understand how the psychological traumas of post-colonial oppression have contributed ipso facto to sentences in our mass media that go on for a very long time and, while paying lip-service to strands of right-on thought such as multi-culturalism, the information superhighway, the corruption inherent in public life and the place of woman's role in society today somehow come to an end without really getting anywhere so that you are left wondering five minutes later what exactly all that was about even though they are followed by punchy, slangy two-word sentences. 'Nuff said.

In this current climate that seeks to airbrush away all diversity of opinion, is it really appropriate to pull Christmas crackers, to sing songs, to "make merry" and to generally "have a good time"? Try telling that to Michael Jackson this Christmas, who we as a society have forced into a mythological straitjacket of seminal iconography, hoping this god/man/child we have entrapped in a celebrity of our own making can begin to explain us to ourselves, even though he has never yet been allowed by us to understand the self that is him. I think it was Roland Barthes who once said something about this sort of thing.

And we as a society killed Marilyn

Monroe and Jimi Hendrix and Diana Ross, all within the twelve months leading up to Christmas. And if Diana Ross is still alive, that's only because she's not yet dead.

You know, I sometimes feel an overwhelming sense of isolation when I look at the fairy on top of the christmas tree, this dumb kid in a tutu sitting astride this huge phallic symbol while beneath her the family unit bickers, strains, fights and crumbles. Ding Dong Merrily On High I don't think — Ding Dong *UN*merrily on High, more like!!! Meanwhile — FACT: every present we give our children only serves to make then sadder. Like, last Christmas in an effort to avoid the crass commercialism that is the Festive Season I decided to carve my child an eco-friendly toy bracelet out of an (organic) raw carrot. As she took it out of its box, I waited for her smiles of joy. Instead, she burst into tears, yet another example of one of society's Christmas victims, pressured by her peer group into cracking up under the fierce whip of institutionalised merriment. So, this Christmas, I'm going to keep it simple and make it an essentially creative process by letting my child carve her own (organic) raw carrot, so at least she'll be able to extract a little personal happiness from the whole present-giving bourgeois socialisation process. Have a Happy Christmas everyone. If you must.

DAMIEN HIRST

Fuck me, I could murder a bloody burger. That was the first thing that came into my head when I woke up one afternoon a couple of months ago. Then I thought: *that's a great name for a work of art.* So I set about creating something pretty fucking fantastic from burgers. Like, first I rang round my friends — or my contemporaries as I call them — and asked all about burgers.

"What are they — vegetables, are they?" I said. "Do they grow in the ground or what?"

"Nah!" they said. "Burgers isn't vegetables they're *meat*, man."

"Meat?" I said. "Meat? But you don't see burgers running round in fields. What are they, then, hedgehogs or something?"

"Nah!" they said. "They're cows!"

"But they're too small for cows, man."

"Nah!" they said. "They cut them up."

"Bloody fucking marvellous," I said. "I'll buy a cow for fifty quid, cut it in half, put one half in one glass cabinet, the other half in another, and sell each half at *exactly the same time* to a different Saatchi." And that's how my latest exhibit, 'Fuck Me, I Could Murder a Burger' came to be created. Don't ask me what it means, I only created it, but to me it's about how people are just babies when they are born, and about how life ends in death, and about how no one can really ever know what's going on in someone else's mind, and, most important of all, it's about

100 grand plus VAT, know what I mean?

You have to be a nutter on some level to do what I do. I mean, basically I'm a bloody nutcase. A bloody fucking great nutcase. Like, I'm a rebel, and I like to stick two fingers up at the Establishment, getting really pissed and telling them the unpalatable truth about life and death and the whole fucking thing.

I went to a dinner party at Charles Saatchi's pad last night. Everyone was there — Lords, Sirs, celebrities, presidents of this and that, toffs, the lot — and I really showed them what's what. First, I drank my champagne in a really surly way — the surliest possible way you can possibly drink champagne — just to show I wasn't taken in by the whole 'glamour' and 'expense' trip. And Lord Linley was there, too, and the Lloyd Webbers. Second, for the first course, which was some sort of fucking pâté, like a human brain all mashed up, I specially used the big knife, which was meant for the main course, and I didn't care who the fuck saw me do it, and this really threw them, this really rubbed their noses in it, because it meant that when the main course came I just used the smaller knife, which was really in 'conventional' terms meant for the fucking pâté. And the President of the Royal Academy was there too. See, in my book, it's the whole purpose of an artist to shock and disconcert, and I can't just stop being an artist because I'm at someone's house having dinner, right? Anyway, the third thing I did to bloody shock them out of their bourgeois complacency was to say "What a load of fucking crap" out loud to myself as I was driving away in my Porsche, and that showed them, that really fucking showed them. Or would have done if they'd been around but luckily they weren't.

I smoke cigarettes — ten or twenty a day. Sometimes even over twenty — twenty-one or twenty-two. And then I stub them out in ashtrays. That's the kind of guy I am.

Dangerous. Unconventional. *Obsessive*. Call me a nutter. Call me a rebel. But first of all call me an **artist**.

Ordinary people — *real* people — understand my work much better than any lah-di-dah critics. They aren't prejudiced, you know. Like, when I was showing my last but one work, 'Mindful of His Reputation The Artist Produces Another Horrible Piece Contemplates His Bank Balance and Temporarily Forgets About Death', which as you know consists of a fresh salmon baked in tin-foil, cut in ten pieces and then eaten, leaving only the bones, an old lady came up and stared at it and stared at it for literally ages and ages so eventually I went up to her, right, and asked what she thought of it. And you know what she said? She looked at me and she said: "Is it meant to be the end of a meal?" That was absolutely fantastic, a totally genuine response to what she saw, with none of that art-world crap, because she saw absolutely what it was all about: we are at the end of a meal, all of us, and the next one hasn't begun yet, and we don't even know what restaurant we're going to get it from, do we? But she didn't have any money, so I had to tell her to piss off out of it. You've gotta have what it takes, if you know what I mean, catalogue on request.

A Load of Bollocks. That's the short title of my next piece, the longer title being 'A Load of Bollocks Going Nowhere, Meaning Nothing, Costing Thousands'. It consists of over three hundred different bollocks from all sorts of animals, including humans — Norman Rosenthal's donated two of his — injected with formaldehyde and formed into a sort of oblong pyramid before being cut in half and mounted. It'll really get them talking and it's already made a lot of people totally re-evaluate their whole concept of what is art and what isn't art. Okay, so most of them decided straightaway it isn't art, but what the fuck, what the bloody fuck.

You know what they call me? They call me the master of the macarb mercabe murkabre, the master of the not very nice, that's what they call me. I've created a whole new deeply disturbing revolution in art and made everyone rethink everything they've ever thought of rethinking because I'm an artist for today, right, and I'm doing things that have never been done before in the whole history of art and if anyone says my stuff's not art, well, I'm sorry but it is, because what I'm doing now is exactly what Marcel Duchamp and that lot was doing seventy years or more ago, so it's part of a bloody seventy-year tradition of deeply disturbing revolution in art, so there. Fuck me, I could murder a bloody burger. Hey, that's great name for a work of art, I'll sell it to my pal Saatchi-boy in the morning, once I've ordered up the corpse and the glue, right?

These We Have Loved

JOHN OSBORNE

Current objects of detestation: divorcees whose bitterness inclines them to defile their espouses with words of self-deceiving ugliness; men with whiskers; arrogant theatrical has-beens who can't understand why famous actors run a mile from their boorish ranting plays; old Garrick Club members who pose for photographs in bowties of a vile purple so as to make themselves look like marvellous old characters; ageing children who can't stand on their own two feet, preferring to blame mummy and all other women for everything; writers so rankly bereft of new ideas that they put their sluggardly hands into smelly bottom drawers in order to rework their tedious past triumphs; touchy old men full of a self-loathing misdirected at others less fortunate than themselves; revolting ranters whose tiny little minds are clogged with the opinions voiced in *The Daily Mail* correspondence columns of twenty years ago.

THE
LAST WORD
TEAM

Germaine Greer: On this page we're going to discuss openly for the first time some truly important questions. Is the Englishman's word still his bond? Is this country going to the dogs? What's happening to us all? Whose life is it anyway? Will you still love me tomorrow? Do you know the way to San Jose? And how much is that doggy in the window, woof woof? Any thoughts, Ann?

Ann Leslie: On the question of the doggy in the window, quite frankly it's a well-known fact that the vast majority of ordinary decent people couldn't give a damn about how much the doggy is, quite frankly, or that it's a doggy at all, and they'd much rather it stayed cooped up in the bloody window, quite frankly, because I've spoken to the vast majority of ordinary decent people and they're bored with the whole thing, thank you very much, quite frankly.

Germaine Greer: Any miserable comments to make at this juncture, Token Sad Woman?

Token Sad Woman: I disagree. I think basically the real problem is that men should be responsive to the needs of women and second basically men should spend less time fussing about what women need and finally it really gets up my nose the way men are always to-ing and fro-ing between living their own lives and trying to live ours. So I agree. And that makes me pretty sad, basically.

Janet Street-Porter: I must say I find it really urgghh when, like, someone goes urgghh and it really makes you feel urgghh. And most of my close friends feel the same, like, urgghh. And while we're on the subject could I just mention two words, since we're all adults: cock and fart?

(ROARS OF LAUGHTER)

Suzanne Moore: Can I just say that men are only good for two things: sex and DIY!

Germaine Greer: Isn't the real problem that everyone is much older these days? I mean, I remember in the sixties, everyone was twenty or so, but now it seems to me that most people are in their fifties with their own chat shows. That means everyone's thirty years older than they were then, and that's kinda frightening, don't you think, Token Twenty-Year-Old?

Token Twenty-Year-Old: Like, okay, I mean, kind of, y'know, like he said, okay, like, y'know, *let's have it off*, right, like and well, it kind of, y'know, really sort of, I mean, well, so I said, okay, right, *let's have it off*, like, y'know.

Suzanne Moore: To my mind, men are only good for two things: sex and DIY!!

Germaine Greer: As we approach the millennium, are we experiencing a major sea-change of perception? Are we dead to all sense of honour, truth, loyalty? Have we forgotten the meaning of words like community and commitment and cohesion? In the year 2525, if man is still alive, if woman can survive, what may they find?

Ann Leslie: I read somewhere that apparently there's this tribe in — I don't know — somewhere like Africa or India or South America, anyway, there's this Arab tribe, probably in China or somewhere, where the women are all happy, and apparently, or so these very distinguished anthropologists say, they really don't like being happy at all — it makes them very, very sad. And that's an absolute fact.

Janet Street-Porter: I'm sorry, but I find that really urgghh, like men are really much smarter than we give them credit for. 'Cept for some of them, who are really much more stupid.

Suzanne Moore: Actually, now I come to think of it, men are only good for two things: sex and DIY!!!

Token Sad Woman: A man I used to know once invited me out to dinner in a smart restaurant. I felt just terrible about it. Before the meal came, he started asking me all sorts of questions, really awful questions like "what would you like to drink?" and "how are you?". So as you can imagine I felt pretty ghastly. Then the waiter — who was also a man — came up, and said something like, "Are you ready to order?". And of course I felt dreadful. And then we had our meal, talked a bit, and left the smart restaurant. I don't know how I coped, but somehow I did. I hope to God I'll never go through an experience like that again, never ever, but my God it taught me a lesson about men.

Token Twenty-Year-Old: Right. Like, I mean, y'know, like if they say **have it off** you either, right, y'know, I mean, yeah, **have it off**, or, like, you don't, y'know, **have it off**, it's kind of up to you whether you **have it off** or not. Or something, like, it's kind of, y'know.

Germaine Greer: Absolutely. We know from statistics that something has happened. Something truly cataclysmic has happened to our society, and everyone agrees on that. But what is it? Nobody seems to know. And that's what perturbs me, it really does. We've got to start asking some important questions. What are we doing to each other? Who am I? What in God's name are we doing here? Where are we exactly? Where did you put the potato peeler? And would you like to ride in my beautiful, my beautiful balloon? Janet, any controversial thoughts?

Janet Street-Porter: Like, there's this bloke I know who sometimes takes off his trousers, right, and then his pants...

(ROARS OF LAUGHTER)

Janet Street-Porter: And underneath it all he has this WILLY!!

(MORE ROARS OF LAUGHTER)

Token Sad Woman: I had this friend once.

Suzanne Moore: Stop me if I've said this already, but I think men are only good for two things: sex and DIY!!!!

Ann Leslie: Apparently there's this tribe in Africa —

Germaine Greer: I'm going to have to stop you there, Ann. Next week, I ask my guests: "What are we all up to?" "Why are we all here?" "What is it all for?" And the question on everyone's lips: "Why can't anyone stop us?"

BERNARD LEVIN

Forsooth, my liege, I may have said it before, and — for these things, as all sane men and women, not to mention children or, for that matter, babes in arms, understand, come in the most circular, roundabout or cyclical of cycles — I have little doubt that I shall, in the course of time (incidentally, I purchased a new watch last week, and what a splendid contraption it is, measurably smaller than a full-blown clock and fitted with a handy little strap for the purpose of securing it to the wearer's wrist, thus affording him the correct time, at a look or glance, throughout his busy, industrious, hard-working, labouring, active day) say it again, but we know precious little about this multifariously spinning globe we term, for the sake of simplicity (and when was simplicity ever forsaken within the portals of this column, may one ask, in a spirit of most humble, as our old chum Mr U. Heep might enunciate it, inquiry?) the world, and that little knowledge of which we can indeed boast — the undoubted excellence, undoubtedly excellent, of a night spent in the most sumptuously comfortable seat at the new (was ever newness such a novelty? was ever novelty so *new*?) Glyndbourne opera house of my very dear friend Mr George Christie of that parish and Mary, perfect chatelaine, whom God preserve, and preserve again, and preserve thrice over, nay a double brace of times, oh, *very well then*, preserve *forever*, all the while feasting, *twixt* arias, upon a serviceable dish, plate, bowl or saucer (though a saucer, forgive me, may be too small, tiny, *petite*, a dish too big, large, extravagant, ostentatious, grandiose for such a task) laden, for preference — my own preference, that is (who else's? you may well ask) — with a goodly selection of gloriously succulent cheeses (I am, I will have you know, a *chevalier de la Confrerie des Tastes-Fromage de France*, and, pshaw, I have a medal to prove it, forsooth, and let no one, neither man nor beast, beast nor man, tell me I haven't, or I will term him an arrant knave and damned bounder to boot and challenge him to pistols at dawn, or in the early morning, whichever renders up the more words upon the page) among them a divinely gooey *Reblochon*, rich and velvety in its almost velvety richness, comparable to the finest *Dairylea*, the perfect accompaniment to, say, Don Giovanni's dying notes, with their ripe overtones of saliva dripping off *foie gras de canard*, washed down with a supremely sticky, fiendishly syrupy and altogether sublimely heavenly *Muscat de Beaumes de Venise*, blissfully reminiscent of Kathleen Ferrier's positively liquid performance in Gluck's *Orfeo*, and the knowledge, doubt thee not, nor, having doubted once, doubt again, that what goes up must, as the philosopher (damned doltish profession) once famously opined, come down, descend, drop, dive, plunge, decline, topple, fall, come a cropper (and admirers of Sir Isaac will be profoundly relieved and encouraged to learn that I entirely agree with him in matters gravitational), yet, if you will kindly settle down, preferably with a stiffish drink in hand, and hear out my present argument, there remains within this world, this globe (what a piece of work is a man! how noble in reason! how infinite in faculty, in form, in moving, how express and admirable! in articles, how capable of plundering the goodly Bard!), this sphere revolving in space (hurrah! I'm almost halfway through my own allotted space!) an immense variety of questions both unanswered and unanswerable, their solution known only to the precious phew I'm over halfway now, their secrets deciphered and maintained by a masterful elite (nothing wrong with elites, mark you, oh my word *no*), among these *questions eternale*, and I will not list them all, though on second thoughts I might, being the age-old riddle, posed in many a dusty tome (I am an inveterate and unashamed bookworm forsooth) óf why did the chicken, free-range or factory-farmed, boiled or grilled, roasted or poached, grain-fed or corn-fed, clucking or unclucking, with a deliciously piquant sauce or without (and, as long as I live, I shall never forget the *Poulet d'Agneau aux Sauce Cerises* I was served in *Monsieur Merdeoc's* fine establishment in the *Bruderholz Allée* in *Basle* in the company of a delicious young lady whose name now, alas, escapes me), cross the road, the lane, the street, the thoroughfare allowing easy (but is anything ever easy? I think not — *thank God*) access to vehicles both authorised and unauthorised, a riddle that, you can bet your bottom dollar, you will have the devil's own job to unravel, if unravel it you seek to do, and one should not lightly set aside the second great riddle, a riddle that has vexed, doth vex and will continue, doubt ye not midshipmen all, to vex Honest Jack Levin, as once it vexed our old friends Socrates and Plato (come to think of it, is there anything in all history to touch the thoughts of those two wise old birds, thoughts so similar in profundity to my own, though ne'er, methinks, so fulsomely express'd?), namely, how can the hard press'd columnist, deadline advancing in time's winged chariot like Coleridge's corn-fed bird of ill omen (Oman, it might interest you to hear, is far from being my favourite country, indeed, it may even benefit you, dear reader, to dip into your groaning wallet full hard and long before sending out your butler to stake that hard earn'd tuppeny-ha'penny with your trusty neighbourhood bookmaker upon a wager that it is among my very *least favourite* of countries), extend his meagre thimbleful of opinions, *apercus*, humorous asides, observations, expressions of dissent, ill-gotten japes, seasoned beliefs, dogmas, convictions, judgements, tenets (call me sissy, but I would prefer, willy-nilly, to sleep between four walls and a ceiling than

ever in a tenet), views, reminiscences, declarations, debates, enthusiasms and arguments in such a way as to fill the vast space allotted by whomsoever decideth upon such infernal matters in the inky recesses of the newspaper in question, and let us thus pause awhile to raise aloft a hearty cheer to that happy band of men — may I include myself? — who have, with one resounding whoop of delight, happened to crack this particular nut, and to whom the secret of spinning out words — nouns, adjectives, verbs, pronouns, even on occasion (ooh! you old devil Levin, you!) adverbs and peradventure conjunctions has been well and truly vouchsafed, for it is a secret — if secret it be, and it most certainly is, or my name is Jack Robinson, which it is not, or was not when last I looked at my birth certificate, which I have not, I should herein admit, for many a long moon — based upon the age-old but alas now long-forgotten art of waffle, waffle repetitive (I repeat — repetitive) and yet strangely forthright, waffle sentimental and soggy, waffle banal and conceited, waffle so brilliantly wound up within itself, a veritable monument of waffle in praise of the waffler, waffle all so perfectly *wafflish*, that forsooth, my liege, I may have said it before, and — for these things, as all sane men and women, not to mention children, or, for that matter, babes in arms, understand, come in the most circular, roundabout or cyclical of cycles — I have little doubt that I shall, in the course of time, think now what was I saying?

DAVID LODGE

How to write as good as what I write like (1): "Creating the Comic Name".

Let's take one example from a recent milestone in comic fiction — *Changing Places* by David Lodge. The main character is a brash American acadaemic. The author had to choose a name for him which would reflect the Jamesian cultural disparity between old/new and England/America to heightened comic effect. The name he finally selected, after a great deal of thought and research, was "Morris Zapp" — a brilliant choice, rich in mimetic and phonetic overtones yet still firmly based in the naturalistic tradition.

Incidentally, in my new novel, I am struggling to think of a suitable name for a small provincial novelist who continually seems to borrow other writers' creations. The name "David" — historically diminutive — might suggest the limits of his talent, but I am now searching for a surname that might subliminally recall his tendency to move in on and live off other people's ready-furnished creations. Any suggestions?

What have been called my "exuberant satirical gifts" and "profound sense of the interactive discourse" have, in recent weeks, been left standing by what, for want of a better word, one must call reality.

For the best part of a year, I had been employing a wide range of critico-creative skills — didactic, modernist, post-modernist, structuropolyphonic, post-Jamesian cultural-historical — in the examination of "The Art of Fiction" for a leading Sunday newspaper. In this notable series, I would instruct readers exactly how novelists such as Fielding, James, Greene and Lodge manage to achieve their authorial effects. For instance, when a novelist of the calibre of, say, Lodge, writes a sentence like:

"I am wonderful," he declared, "and my books are serio-comic masterpieces"

I would examine how the authorial voice captures such an exuberant and authentic tone of quasi-acadaemic self-promoting smugness in just one short sentence. In one of these masterclasses, I chose one outstanding modern novel — Lodge's *Nice Work* — and showed how, by a process of almost intangible textual assimilation acquiring a range of literary skills, parodic, historic, comic, ironic, spasmodic, Lodge was able to cross-relate with the plot of a Victorian novel — Gaskell's *North and South* — and, by placing it in a modern context, to explore a variety of literary, psychological and socioeconomic themes, all to telling effect. Result: *a highly original and imaginative use of post-modernist literary cross-reference.*

I then revealed that a vastly lesser-known novelist, a female whose work had so far failed to win her any plaudits whatsoever from cultural or literary critics, had come by the plot for her latest potboiler. She had simply borrowed large chunks of the plot of Gaskell's *North and South*, repositioning it against a modern background. Result: *out-and-out plagiarism by an obscure writer revealing a marked lack of originality and imagination.*

And this is where the plot becomes as amusing and unpredictable as a novel by, say, Lodge. The obscure and unimportant female "novelist" reveals that she has been plunged even further into obscurity. Meanwhile, the critically-acclaimed, prize-winning novelist known for his exuberant satirical gifts continues to grow more and more successful. Which all goes to show that, as I once mentioned in my series of international lectures, "Mimesis and Diagesis in Modern Fiction", happy endings can occur in life as well as in literature!

How to write as good as what I write like (2):"Nodding Towards Current Theory".

Let's take a look at a ground-breaking comic novel: say, *Funny Old Life* (1986) by David Lodge. Ostensibly, this is a novel about acadaemic "A" entering the life of acadaemic "B" and vice-versa — and all to brilliantly rich comic effect! But the genius of *Funny Old Life* — and the reason the critics seemed to like it so much — is that, to use techno-critical phraseology, it "nods" at fashionable theories relating to deconstructionism and post-modernism and decomposition without ever letting them "get in the way". Thus, five paragraphs from the end of chapter 5, the authorial voice wonders whether he was right to name the main character "Morris" rather than "Horace" or "Boris". Such a device undermines the normal kind of authority which a text claims, conveying a dislocating sense of self-questioning provisionality, greatly appealing to the acadaemic reader. But after two sentences, the authorial voice considers that "Morris" was the correct choice all along, and the story proceeds in rollicking style right up to the side-splitting conclusion, when "B" realises he has more in common with "A" than perhaps he originally thought!! Result: critics and readers are happy, and *Funny Old Life* goes into a ninth impression.

Let's shift the discourse. What makes a novelist really comic? It's usually a mixture of incongruitive disparities within interactive fictive arenas, but of course in my case it's the hairstyle.

The Chief Stylist for Penguin Books hit upon the notion of giving me a greasy-haired acadaemic fringe circa 1971 as a way of visually signifying, in the Barthian sense, that, to employ an idiomatic speech-formula, "The Author-Figure as a Complete Nerd", an acronym, the inhouse semiologists tell me, for Neo-Exegetic Reactive Deconstructionist.

Since then, my sales worldwide have shot up, partly because, the statisticians tell me, up to 40% of my most devoted readers think that I am in fact Chris de Burgh, creator of "Lady in Red" and many other chart-topping melodies. Topped off with some brand-new flared rust-coloured cords and a new, wry, knowing look on my dust-jackets, by the mid-Nineties I am hoping to be internationally acknowledged as the most comic novelist around.

How to write as good as what I write like (3): "Creating an Imaginary World".

Two major 20th century British novelists — Bradbury (b. 1932) and Lodge (b. 1935) —have created an imaginary tragic-comic world in which two Professors on the international lecture circuit write comic novels about the self-absorption of Professors on the international lecture circuit and then pay generous tribute on the international lecture circuit to each other's comic novels about the self-absorption of the international lecture circuit. Stretching the boundaries of the novel is what good writing's all about, and for this I proudly salute them.

LINDA McCARTNEY

Hi. Let's groove. Whenever folk drop round to our house, which isn't big at all, it's really quite small, I welcome them with a carrot. Then I say. "Would you like that cooked?"

That's a test question. It's how I've come to be such a sensitive judge of other people, stripping the outer fabric off to lay bare the inner soul. 'Cos if they reply: "Yes, I'd like this carrot cooked, please, Linda". I know the kind of person they are.

"OUT!" I say, "Out, you carrot-murderer! I won't let my children near somebody who throws a poor little carrot into BOILING WATER! OUT! OUT! OUT! Bad vibes! Bad vibes! OUT!" It's only by sticking to these basic human principles that I've managed to achieve my inner serenity.

All my life, I've been on a great voyage of discovery towards innocence and beauty. You see, I love life. Some mornings, I get up real early and I get in our car — not a big car, I've seen lots bigger, I'd even call it very small compared to some I've seen — and I go into town, searching for carrots that have been dug up from their lovely homes in the ground. Often these carrots have had their beautiful green hair cut off, and have been bundled together — can you *believe* it? — in a horribly constricting non-organic plastic bag just awaiting painful immersion in boiling water. So I say to their jailer/shopkeeper: "I want to release these carrots, I don't care what it costs, man" and then I hand over however much money it takes.

When I get home, I set the carrots loose in one of the very small woods we own. And do you know? Sometimes I can hear them whisper back in carrot-language, "Thank you, Linda you're a really beautiful free spirit" out of their little carrot mouths.

Top Tips for Meaningful Photos (1): Always Remember to Put Film in the Camera.

The reason I have become so famous and well-reputed is that I have almost always remembered to put film in my camera, even in the Sixties, when most photographers seemed to be into a forgetting trip. That way, you can be sure that when it comes to unload the film, there'll be a film there to unload.

I used to love photographing Keith Moon, the madcap drummer of The Who. Moony was one of the shyest, quietest and sensitivest people I ever met, and his way of expressing it was to be really loud-mouthed, gregarious and insensitive. I may have been the only person who really understood him. I think he really hated beating those drums so hard, night after night. Drums have feelings too, you know. Perhaps it led to his early death. Moony used to like me. He always said that if ever he felt the need to puke over somebody, he really hoped it would be me.

Paul and I are really into being normal. We're both very anti the whole material thing. We're happy with very little, and maybe that's why we have so much. I mean, what do people really need? A roof over their heads, vegetables, proudness for their family, a yard where the kids can run around and maybe one or two counties and a few islands, nothing more.

At the moment, Paul and I are really into riding on public transport, we think it's really hip. We don't make a big thing about it, we're not into the whole celebrity trip, we just pay the dough for the bus and drive it away, probably to our Scottish estate, which is very small, especially when you compare it to

Canada or Africa. We're so into public transport that now we've got ten buses lined up outside the croft. They love it there, sitting out in the blowy, blowy wind with mind-expanding views over the heather and moorland. And I'll tell you something. The reason they are still with us is because they like what I feed them, which is lovely Linda's own vegan mixture of grass and water. We don't allow petrol in our family. It's a product of oil, which is formed of lots of little fossils of dead animals. And anyway, once our buses have tasted grass and water, I'm telling you, they won't go anywhere else.

Top Tips for Meaningful Photos (2): Keep Still.

If you move your camera around too much, the photos can become kind of blurred. Same with the subject. Always make sure you choose a subject which is as still as possible, like carrots, or rock stars. In the sixties, I was really into photographing rock stars. In a way, my camera was my musical instrument, only it wasn't a musical instrument, it was my camera. My favourite subjects were Janis Joplin, Jimi Hendrix, Keith Moon, Mama Cass and Jim Morrison. Sometimes it seemed like they could keep still for weeks on end, even years. Incredible days, The Sixties. We all really got off on the energy.

As I say, I'm a musician, only with my camera. If you're an artist, you treat all instruments just the same. For instance, I play keyboard exactly the same way I take photographs. Like, if I'm on stage with Paul, I stand behind the keyboards, and I press each button down, very carefully one by one at five minute intervals, just as I would my camera, and if I get it wrong first time, I press it again and again until I get it right. You know, Paul loves what I do to those keyboards so much he wants my music to become even more organic and real and upfront and true, and so for our next gig he's gonna see that I play completely natural, without it being plugged in and out-vibed by electricity. I can really relate to that.

Top Tips for Meaningful Photos (3): Communicate.

To truly communicate, you need innocence. Picasso was probably thinking of me when he said the true artist must never lose her innocence. I want to be as innocent as a cabbage running wild in the forests, as a fish grazing in the meadow, or an oyster as he chirps his merry tune from high upon the mountain ledge. Sometimes, I think I might be really too innocent for this world. "La la la la la la the lovely Linda".* Yeah, Paul really got to the heart of us both in that song. He expressed something about our lack of materialistic craving, about our freedom from worldly ambition, about our famous normalcy, our hatred of the whole "ownership" thing. Sing songs! Make pictures! Forget about tomorrow! Love Life! Groove!

(*Reproduction of all or part of this lyric without permission and full prior payment to Eastman McCartney Business Associates International Inc. still result in immediate prosecution under the safeguard of copyright act.)

ROBERT NEWMAN & DAVID BADDIEL

Rob: Like, Christ, yeah, right. Who wants to read this anyway?!! Talk about crap. Okay. Here we go then. Right. The comedy starts here!

Stonehenge. What a crap building. Hasn't even got a ceiling. If it was like your place you couldn't take a girl back there and shag her arse off because you'd get covered in rain. That's if it was raining, of course. Not to mention like the tourists. I mean, for fuck's sake, who wants to shag the arse off a girl in front of loads of like total prats?!!

Dave: Classic monologue, really classic, Dave. Like, when people say that our comedy is puerile, that it's just a load of wank, I want to point them in the general direction of our literally amazing classic comic monologues like the one Dave's just done on Stonehenge. We don't just DO comedy, no, we USE comedy to challenge our audience's basic preconceptions about really dark, deep subjects like the human attitude to history, and to sex, and to notions of privacy. Like Rob's really obsessed with genuine misery and loneliness, and our comedy reflects these concerns and by like doing so it makes all our viewers feel, well, really kind of lonely and miserable.

Personally, I'm obsessed by death and old age and I really believe that if you can be funny about things like death and old age like you're actually helping people to feel better about them. Here's an example, one of our all-time classics: "Christ, my old grandad died at 95 last week. Served him right for trying to shag the arse off his zimmer frame — like I always knew he was a short-sighted piss-artist, but I thought that was going a bit far!!!"

See what I mean? Holding on to your sense of childishness — or childlikeness, more like — is what great comedy's all about. Through that joke, me and Rob say far more about old age, and the tragedy of death, and the futility of human aspiration, and the basically non-stop quality of decay than say someone like T.S. Eliot ever managed in any of his paintings.

Rob: Right. Our material relaxes that desperately personal grip people have on life's problems and lets them know they're not alone in their misery. Like, another reason Stonehenge is such a crap building —

Dave: Note the running joke!!!

Rob: — Is that it's got well tons of holes in its walls — like, you couldn't hang your poster of Nirvana or The Sundays any-bloody-where because it would keep falling down, like, because even what walls there are are all like crumbley — in fact, it's piss-awful!!!

Dave: Classic! I'll tell you what really bugs me, right, is like all these tossers who say we're like just using old material and performing it really crappily and mixing it with words like spunk and wank and poofters and that somehow by doing this we're gaining street cred with teenagers who don't know any better because they're inarticulate and full of wanky shit like us. Well what total crap but total and utter wank. We're nothing like other comedians because other comedians just make people laugh — ha, ha, ha, ho, ho, ho, etcetera — but we don't just make people laugh, in fact we don't make them laugh at all, we're the most serious comedians who've ever like existed, and, like if we raised a smile we'd regard it as well, pretty crappy really — like a girl you've just been shagging the arse off going really spare on you, and comparing your penis to a gherkin when you always thought it was more of a marrow!

Rob: Right! In my opinion, comedy is all like about you know thingy.

Dave: Timing.

Rob: Right, yeah — and the other thing too, you know, whatsitcalled?

Dave: Delivery?

Rob: Yeah, and that's what I was going to say, like other comedians have crap delivery and crap thingy. But not us. And talking of crap what a crap place Stonehenge turned out to be — I mean, it might be historic and built by some Roman bloke and all that but where's the CD cabinet, then?!!! I really feel like playing some Guns n' Roses, but I couldn't do that, not at Stonewankyhenge.

Dave: And don't talk to me about Almighty God — what a toss-artist he turned out to be!! And Mohammed? What sort of name is Mohammed? Buddha, too: I wish I had as many willies as he had arms — and so do my attractive girlfriends!!

Rob: Seriously, though: with jokes like that we're encouraging people to take a long hard look at themselves and their religion, and to find their own particular path towards the ultimate truth, if any.

Dave: Did you say "the ultimate poof"?!!! Well, I'll put on another pair of trousers, then — because I like shagging the arse off birds, not blokes!!

Rob: A friend of mine came by you know like the other night and I let her in you know and she said, the thing is, I haven't brought a punchline. So I said, well, you know, don't bother, like, 'cos neither have I but they'll probably go mental about it anyway and laugh their arses off because like they're usually too thick to notice one way or the other.

Dave: Classic. Our humour's intensely internal, not like everybody else's. Like, I make jokes like, "God, I'm so miserable and rejected that I feel like one of those bits that looks like snot that gets put on a saucer in the fridge by some girl you've had around the house shagging your arse off and it's like, the comedy of recognition, because everyone who's been in that position recognises it and they don't feel so intensely isolated any more.

Hey, Rob, see that pile of doggy-poo over there?

Rob: Yeah, Dave.

Dave: That's our act, that is.

CAMILLE PAGLIA

What d'you mean, who's *she*? Okay. Okay. It might not be what you said, but it was what you were thinking, right? *Right?* Who's she, my ass. Who's she my fucking ass. She's only CAMILLE PAGLIA, the world-class intellectual, internationally renowned — and also in Japan — for her supreme skills as a thinker, researcher and writer, the woman who's brought a new level of dignity to the world of American scholarship, so stuff you if you don't know who I am, fuckass. B-i-i-i-g *deal*! And what the fuck do you know about dignity, anyways, twitface? You wouldn't know culture if it came up and cut your balls off, slutass.

My huge, brilliantly intelligent, world-famous *magnus opus* and great work, *Sexual Personae* — buy it, *pigface* — turned me into a timeless, almost Apollonian world figure, almost as big as, like, Keith Richards. Of course, the wimps and sluts and castratoes and fatsoes on the pathetically mediocre Ivy League campuses just didn't, like, comprehend my intellect, they're so bound up with their own screwy little worlds, but I find that the blacks and the hispanics I meet in the laundrettes and discos downtown, the crack-dealers on the streets and the Puerto Rican prostitutes in the gutters, the *real* people I mix with, not the prissy little ass-kissing eunuchs in Harvard and Yale, have no problem relating to my revolutionary ideas on the nature of Sophoclean tragedy, none at all. *Whoooo!* You can feel that intellectual *energy* rise up in you when your body's close to a big black guy, real sweaty, and you're swapping notes on Nietzsche, know what I mean? Oh my *Gaaaad!* Even flicking through Walter Pater's got nothing on *that!*

My lasting achievement as a cultural critic and — *face it, fatface* — genius has been to place the American popular culture of today in its proper 10,000-year context, linking the artistic icons of the moment with the geniuses of the past. I was, like, the very first critic to notice the similarity of spiritual conflict and thwarted artistic ambition between Caravaggio and Yogi Bear, for instance, and my pioneering recognition of the cross-fertilisation between the tangential uncertainties of Brahms' 1st Symphony (1876) and the chorus of David Cassidy's revoltingly underrated "How Can I Be Sure?" (1972) has drawn me many, many plaudits from the one living scholar and thinker who really matters, Professor Paglia of the University of Arts, Table Tennis and Domestic Science in Philadelphia, USA.

You know what? I owe one helluva lot to Ludwig van Wittgenstein — and vice-versa. Like me, he was no schmuck, and I can relate to that, but, like, I kind of think he never really knew the meaning of the word *boooogie*, you know what I mean? Like, he wasn't *h-i-i-p*. Gaaaad! — I bet he probably couldn't name more than three hit records by Madonna!!! And, like, what did the Tractatus Schmactatus ever tell us about *Star Trek*? Get down and get with it, Ludwig! But like Canaletto, Joan Collins and Shakespeare — another three great influences on my imagination — he will always be remembered as a major force in my intellectual development. But you know who I really hate? You know who I really, really hate and *detest?* Bertrand Russell! Don't mention that man's name to me! I said, *don't mention it!* Talk about Wimpsville! Some philosopher he turned out to be! When did he ever get a full colour photograph of himself dressed up in full leather gear with his cleavage bursting out onto page 27 of *Vanity Fair*? Never! Well, stuff you, Bertrand — Paglia has! Philosopher? Puh-*leez!* That guy's no philosopher! No *w-a-a-a-y!* He couldn't philosoph half as well as what I can!

Let's get a coupla things clear, okay? I said, okay?? Much as I respect the sincerely held beliefs of the feminist lobby — fat sluts and skinny neuros — I will not, repeat NOT allow them to simplistically caricature my beliefs in a personal vendetta to further their own disgusting blathering dykey opportunistic hangdog dowdie ends.

Contrary to the lies and distortions put out by my enemies, I am not an anti-feminist, in fact I'm the greatest feminist of them all, I'm a pioneering feminist, a fully-fledged feminist, a feminist beacon to all future generations, dammit. In fact, I'm *soooo* feminist that I hate women to pieces and I think the whole history of Western civilisation from Socrates to Bon Jovi proves that men are one helluva lot better at everything except for maybe, like, some specialised areas of macrame. Which is not to say that I'm a woman. I'm not. I see myself as more a one-off, a feminine man in a woman's body with a woman's masculinity, a man's brain and a woman's desire for peace and stability, got it, fat-face?

And guess what. Yep. They've caricatured my position on rape, totally caricatured it, totally, totally but *TOTALLY*. Totally. I never said anything about rape being fun, I never said date-rape's no crime. No w-a-a-a-y did I say those terrible things. What I actually said about it was "wild, infectious delirium of gang rape" (*Newsday*, 1991) and "We cannot legislate what happens on a date. Sex is a dangerous sport" (CNN, 1991) which is totally, totally but *TOTALLY* not the same, and to say different is personally insulting to me as a scholar, a thinker, a philosopher and a writer of world renown so I wish those neurotic crybabies and titless crapartists would, like, just go fuck themselves, that's what I say!

Let's talk about me for once. I feel I have to, you know, because as far as I can tell no one in the whole civilised world is talking of anything else. I even heard that Barbra Streisand mentioned my name to Nick Nolte the other day, God's truth, and Andy Williams is a b-i-i-i-g fan too, and so's Whitney Houston, or so I'm told. And Perry Como was knocked out by what I wrote about John Jack Rousseau, who, let me tell you, was the real precursor of Acid House, along with Byron, of course, whose influence can also be appreciated on a broader scale in the early episodes of *Knott's Landing*. Lacan, Derrida, who needs them? Fuck off, Foucault, that's what I say! *Whoooo! Woweee! Ramadamadingdong!* PAGLIA's here, and she's gonna turn America into a truly cultured, intellectual and, like, *civilised* nation, with or without your fucking help, asshole!

MICHAEL PALIN

*N*orth Pole. This really is an extremely cold place, with ice absolutely everywhere! It's at the very top of the world — or bottom, depending on which way you're looking at it! As I say, my main impression of it is of its great chilliness: literally indescribable!

When you contrast it with some of the places I'm due to visit — the deserts, for instance, or parts of Africa — well, you can only stop and wonder at how very cold it is! Certainly one of the coldest places I have ever been by quite a long way — including Chipping Sodbury in November!

Actually, it's Pythonesque jokes like that one — Chipping Sodbury in November! — that keep one's spirits up, out here at the top (or bottom!) of the world, all alone by oneself amidst all this ice, with nothing and no one for company but the ice and the freezing cold and the grey skies and the camera crew and the sound recordists and the producer and the director and the researchers and let's not forget the travel co-ordinator. Frankly, the sense of solitude is literally indescribable.

*O*dessa. I visit the Odessa Steps: lots and lots of steps, named after Odessa. Odessa is one of the very few cities I can think of which begin with an "O" — unless you count Orpington! Actually, it's rather like Orpington in a way: there are lots of buildings, and quite a few people, plus cars and so on. As cities go, Odessa is literally indescribable.

Before I came here, I had no idea how big Russia is. It really is very, very big indeed. The people here are very friendly. Today, after quite a comfortable night, it has been my privilege to meet a marvellous old character, a gentleman who speaks near-perfect English, dresses very smartly in suit and tie, has heard of the Pythons (always a help!) and is anxious to co-operate in any way he can. "We must get him on film — he's a marvellous old character," I say to my producer.

"He's actually our assistant director," says my producer.

Later, I rehearse the next day's script. "I must say this view is simply stunning," I say over and over again. Tomorrow, we will find a view to go with it.

*R*hodes. I must say, this view is simply stunning. This is a truly magical place, a city full of almost Pythonesque contrasts: very colourful and full of real character, very much like some English towns, in some ways more so and in some ways rather less so! Strolling around Rhodes — which incidentally has rather fewer "roads" than Birmingham! — I breathe in its character: truly magical, and full of — almost Pythonesque! — contrasts.

Always on the look out for humour, I bump into one old boy who quite literally can't speak a word of English, and has no idea who I am! We get the camera crew assembled, and sure enough he makes a great interviewee, not understanding a word I say, thus allowing me to do a variety of funny faces to camera!

Before I arrived here, I had no idea how big Rhodes was. I must say, upon further investigation its actual size is really quite surprising. But why, I wondered, does it have that mysterious "h" in its name? No-one could tell me!

*A*swan. After a slightly uncomfortable night, I wake up. I pay a trip to the famous Aswan dam, an extraordinary feat of engineering, dealing with a lot of water every day of the year. This is a very colourful country, full of hidden secrets never vouchsafed to the outsider. I ask one of the locals — quite a character — what it is like to live in Aswan. He tells me he enjoys it quite a lot. "I imagine that the difference between living in Aswan and living in England is literally indescribable," I say. He mentions that he doesn't know, as he has never lived in England.

"Do you have a funny hat I can wear for the cameras?" I ask him, but he hasn't got one, so my researcher slips out and buys one — a very Pythonesque garment! I put it on beside the Aswan dam, and make a quip — "It's not unlike wearing a dead parrot!" and the camera crew creases up! In the afternoon, I bid a fond farewell to an utterly magical country, full of a great many contrasts.

*K*hartoum. Another place with an "h" in an odd place in its name! I suppose that's just my somewhat Pythonesque, surreal way of looking at things! After a very comfortable night, I meet some marvellous old characters in the main square of the town. "Do you enjoy it here?" I ask them. "Yes," they reply. I come away with the firm impression that they enjoy it here.

Africa is a vast country, with great distances between one spot and another — far greater than the distance between, say, Nuneaton and East Croydon! Still, you've got to laugh. It's only by taking this humorous approach to things that one can see the world for what it is — a vast sort of globe, full of all sorts of places which might be fun to visit.

After some highly concentrated investigation by your intrepid traveller, I discover that "Khartoum" is not in fact the place where the "Cartoon" was invented. My fellow-Python Terry Gilliam will be much distressed by this news, methinks!

In the evening, after filming me wearing a totally barmy hat a researcher picked up somewhere, we watch the sun setting over the horizon: a literally indescribable sight.

*V*ictoria Falls. This must be one of the wettest places I've been to in a long, long time — wetter even than Droitwich in January, and that's saying something!

Victoria Falls was named after Victoria — though it's not known whether she actually fell or not! Every day, year in, year out, literally masses of water goes over the high rocks, creating an amazing waterfall, formed of lots of water. Certainly a sight to remember, and almost Pythonesque in its total unexpectedness. Somewhere, a long way away, people are doing sensible things like watching cricket or gardening — and here am I standing beside the Victoria Falls wearing a daft hat for the cameras! Makes you think!

*C*ape Town. After a comfortable night, I have a good breakfast and tidy up my room before changing my shoes. On the way out of the hotel, I leave my key with the lady at the desk. I then spend a day looking around South Africa. What a day! Indescribable. Back at the hotel, I pick up my key and prepare for bed. Next stop: The South Pole.

*S*outh Pole. This really is an extremely cold place, with ice absolutely everywhere! It's at the very bottom of the world — or top, depending on which way you're looking at it!

*M*y voyage is finally over. My lasting impression is that the world is full of colour and contrasts, and of all sorts of different people and places. After five months of quality filming from Pole to Pole (plug!) for good old "Auntie Beeb", I know one thing for sure: this whole wide world of ours is quite literally indescribable. Cheerio!

ANTHONY POWELL

20th January 1995: V. and I attended pre-luncheon drinks with the Somersets at Gloucester. Then on to the Gloucesters in Somerset. The Devonshires had brought Kent along. Halfway through luncheon, the butler informed us that Lady Avon was at the door. "Tell her to join us!" said Gloucester, drawing up a chair for her. She sat down and was halfway through her main course (medaillons de veau, pommes Lyonnaises, epinards a la creme — all perfectly eatable), entertaining us with fulsome praise of a new lemon-scented shower gel, whatever that may be, when it emerged that the butler had misheard. She was not the Lady Avon at all, but the Avon Lady. "Surely I might interest you gents in two-in-one apple shampoo and conditioner?" she asked as she was escorted to the door. Quite intolerable. The claret was not unenjoyable.

In the afternoon, re-read complete works of Graham Greene. Pretty thin stuff. Deeply unpleasant fellow, and, one feels, highly conceited: he loathed handing out praise to his contemporaries, retaining all his warmest approval for his own works. Later re-read various fan letters confirming that I am the leading novelist of my generation. Why is it, one wonders, that my fans are so unusually percipient? Or is it the other way round, and do the unusually percipient tend to be my fans? One of life's deeper questions. Must explore further.

21st January 1995: Re-read *Hamlet* by Shakespeare, a competent but unreliable author, though now rather dated and always prone to wordiness. Never to my knowledge managed a novel. Hamlet is a not uninteresting play, but the plot is flawed. The Danes are really extremely minor Royalty, even by Scandinavian standards; scarcely worth a lengthy play. Tremendous hoo-ha in final scenes, characteristic of a particular sort of empty kettle Dane. Prince Hamlet wouldn't have lasted long in Pratt's, where Danish Royalty is taken with a fairly hefty pinch of salt. 'Hamlet', a peculiar name — any relation, one wonders, to the Fotherington-Hamlets of Much Hadham? Much to-ing and fro-ing with ghosts, incest, madness and so forth — always the sign of a writer grasping at straws. I would guess that Shakespeare stole many of his more notable lines from the immortal titles in my own *Dance to the Music of Time* sequence. But I should hate to pass judgement.

22nd January 1995: I received a telephone call from a Professor Wildenstein at Princeton University. He wanted to give me a large amount of money. This is the sort of thing the Americans do very well. He said that I was to be awarded some literary prize or other worth 50,000 dollars, and would I do him the honour, etc, of accepting it. Really the most awful bore, but I suppose one must humour these types. Reluctantly, I accept, wondering why he could just have posted it to me, without the need for 'acceptance'. Needless to say, he was delighted. I have noticed in the past that many Americans pronounce 'Dance' with a sharp 'a', rather than a long 'a'. Have others noticed this too, or is it my novelist's ear? I ask him to send the cheque, but, please, no accompanying letter, as these congratulatory missives can prove tedious to plough through.

Re-read the poems of W.B. Yeats. Very Irish.

Noted that the gentleman who played the drums in the celebrated English popular music group 'Slade' is called Don Powell, suggesting he springs from Spanish nobility. May well be related through the Lloyds of Cordoba (one of whom was a Powell of the Radnorshire house of Holder, which is — intriguingly — also the name of the lead singer). Could also be related by marriage to my sister Margaret, author of *Below Stairs* and other successful volumes of memoirs.

23rd January 1995: Attended luncheon at Buckingham Palace. Unexciting guests, mainly philosophers, writers, artists, with a smattering of politicians and showbusiness types. Infinitely dreary. Valiantly trying to inject a little life into the gathering, I raised the interesting question of the knee in literature. 'Tolstoy is sparing with his knees, Dickens mentions them only rarely, and Jane Austen not at all," I began. "Can anyone think of any great knee passage in English literature?" This question was met by a fascinated silence, so I enlarged upon the point. "It is an aberration of modern times that so often the 'k' in knee is kept silent. It is a perfect example of contemporary vulgarity that so many younger people — "television newscasters" and so forth — choose to go for the awful pronunciation 'nee', with a soft 'k'. But I am delighted to say that the upper classes continue to pronounce it with its 'k' intact. Incidentally, has anyone read the latest 'Eton College Chronicle'? Any good?"

Alas, they were far too dimwitted to tackle such subtle points. By the time I had completed my speech I found they had decamped to a neighbouring room. The wine was Britvic '95. Chateau new to me, slight whiff of orange about it, not at all bad.

Re-read complete works of Dostoievsky. Heavy going. He completely misses the essential light touch that he might have picked up had be been born in England and sent to, say, Eton. Characters lack *bounce*. But I should hate to pass judgement.

24th January 1995: Re-read the latest *Burke's Peerage*. Very sound on what makes a decent human being, much better in that respect than the *Testaments*, Old and New, which may well be perfectly good when dealing with Middle-Eastern Royalty — particularly acute on King David and family — but otherwise absurdly over-rated, allotting far too much space to Jewish families of little or no significance — shepherds, fishermen, tax-collectors, even carpenters — while ignoring many more distinguished families of the time. These include my illustrious forebears, the Pow-Ells of Gomorrah. Ezekiel Pow-Ell was among the most distinguished manufacturers of crosses in his day; one of his companies may well have fashioned the cross that is pivotal to the whole story, yet he is ruthlessly excluded from the text. In my view, the writers of the Gospels made a mistake in concentrating on the rather thin, disruptive (possibly Leftish? Balliol?) character of the Lord Jesus Christ (the name implies he was the younger son of a Duke, but I find no mention of him in *Burke's*) to the exclusion of those from the better families at the wedding feast at Cana.

Re-read Huckleberry Finn. Very American.

CRAIG RAINE

1944: It's a Poet

Baby like hedgehog but
without those pointy bits:
quills. That's it. Quills.

Baby unbearded
as yet, pushes head-first
out of his mummy's pink dressing womb

Like Neil Armstrong
leaving Apollo 9. Or
quite like it, in a way.

Though obviously
Apollo 9 was made of
some sort of metal

And wasn't pink
and it had a control panel
with wires, buttons, levers and so on.

Still one mustn't be
pernickety
when it comes to poetry.

Congratulations, madam,
says the doctor, dressed all
in white, like a

doctor. It's a poet!
A minor poet! Neat on
similes, but we're still checking the

scansion. Baby still
unbearded suckles at
his mother's telephone receiver.

Actually, not her telephone receiver
but her bosoms.
Only they look slightly like

A telephone receiver
as seen from
an unusual angle.

Joyce, Eliot, Pound,
Pasternak, Conrad, Auden,
I thought I'd just

mention them. And also
Haile Selassie and Haile
Mills. And what about

Stalin too? These names
give the poem a swanky ring,
n'est ce pas?

1958: Sprouts

Hair begins to sprout
from the poet's skin
in particular

Around his Eiffel
Tower: non-swanks, it
really is that

big. Also from his
chin and around his mouth
the hairiest poet since

Walt Whitman or
Hendrix, Jimi. Mmmmm,
so modern, so very

Modern. Now,
where was I?
Ah, yes. Hitler

Bombs Bristol while
Grandpa Raine brushes his
piano key teeth

In nearby Oxford. Or at
least quite nearby, if
you take the M4.

1972: The Poet Takes a Pupil
"Hello" he opened
his pillar-box mouth and
let himself in.

"My name's Amis. Martin
Amis. This your
sock is it then?"

Sock! We speak the same
language! For sock
read office! Great minds!

It must have been something
like this when Wordsworth met
Coleridge. I could murder a

Gitanes, Sam. The biff biff war in
Vietnam continues as
Amis learns at the

Poet's elbowish knee.
And look who Amis
knows! Amis knows

Fenton who knows Barnes who
knows McEwan who knows Motion
who knows Shakespeare

Though not to speak to. The
Shah falls. People die like
goldfish. The Ayatollah,

also bearded, sits in the
Peacock over-throne as the
Poet eases into his Faber sock.

1985: Another dirty bit to keep you reading

Anna Vladimirovna Romanovna
naked. Her breasts unfishy shell-
fish now unshelled.

The poet's great grandpa
naked. His leg of
lamb at the ready.

A condom like a
hot air balloon
only smaller.

Spermatozoa wriggling
on the linoleum like
spilt rice pudding.

Whoops. The poet's
great grandpa has
blown it. Sorry, Anna, love.

1994: Oxford. Major work ahead
The world talks of
nothing else. "Read all
about it!" yell

The newsvendors. "Major new
work by Raine!" Crowds
like the collective name for

lots of people stream
from every corner
anxious for an epic

verse history of
Europe, highly praised
by Fenton, Amis,

Raine, Barnes, Raine, Motion,
Raine, McEwan, Raine, Carey,
Morrison, Raine, Raine and

Raine, Raine go away
come again another
thingummy.

WILLIAM REES-MOGG

As I was being shaved yesterday morning, I found myself reflecting that no English monarch since the death of Edward III can be put quite in the first class, though Queen Elizabeth I was undoubtedly sound, and Queen Victoria very nearly Beta Plus. And what of God? Though His mind is too eclectic to be considered truly first-rate, He may still be justly credited with one or two good ideas, the Rees-Mogg family being just one example. We stretch back twelve centuries to Ras Mag, the distinguished President of the Ancient Pict Chamber of Commerce, and a notably successful Vice-Chairman of the Woad Preservation Society. To we Rees-Moggs, Windsor Castle is a comparatively modern, somewhat — dare I say it — *nouveau riche* building, as are its present tenants. But I still incline to the point of view that it should be rebuilt. Life itself is not unlike Windsor Castle: sturdy yet fragile, admitting visitors yet essentially private, permanent yet strangely temporary.

As I grow older, I find myself taking up interests that, in my youth, I might well have eschewed as immature. Until last week, for instance, I had never felt the need to tie my own shoelaces, finding it more convivial to employ someone else for the purpose. The Moggs, true to their Somerset blood, have never set much store by the base technicalities of existence. Consequently the art of tying a shoelace was one I never learned. As a child for a short while, and then as Editor of *The Times*, Vice Chairman of the BBC, Chairman of the Arts Council and later Deputy Chairman of the Milk Marketing Board, I found that employing someone else for the chore saved me time I could usefully spend on re-reading and improving the great works of Peruvian literature.

But in Wessex we have a particular love of walking, and this, last Sunday, was to prove my — and my shoelaces' — undoing. As I was perambulating in a meadow, reflecting that Edward Heath might still be Prime Minister to this day if only he had followed my advice on the Gold Standard, I noticed to my horror that my right shoelace was utterly undone.

What was I to do? My Latin education — even my Presidency of the Oxford Union and later Vice-Presidency of the Mother's Union, followed by a holiday job as Chairman of the World Bank — had not prepared me in any way for this fearful eventuality. It seems to me that Plato, for all his admirable efforts in other fields, teaches us little about shoelaces. At first, I attempted to stumble on, but in so doing fell face downwards into a circular pool of mud, marking the spot where a cow had been recently standing. I then fiddled with the laces, but found that my mind existed on too high a plane to be able to deal with such hapless threads.

At last, the solution came to me: I removed my trousers, tore them neatly in two, and then knotted each trouser leg around each shoe. Though slightly bumpy, my walk back was hugely enjoyable and enlivened by a fine breeze circulating around my legs and upper regions. Henceforth, I will be urging the present Cabinet when next they come to see me to do away with shoelaces. This will have the effect of taking our minds off the recession, and so sterling will recover in no time at all. In many ways, life is like a great shoelace, useful only when done up, standing for what it stands for, a solid yet impermanent knot.

Wittgenstein was no intellectual, and only a second-rate brain, but in many ways he was the superior of Sartre, who was partly intellectual, but a third-rate brain, and roughly the equal of Russell, who was almost certainly an intellectual, but a fourth-rate brain. It is telling, though, that not one of these three men rose to the position of Chairman of the Broadcasting Standards Council: history teaches us that the combination of an intellectual with a first-rate brain is notoriously hard to find.

I have known a great many powerful and learned men in my time, none, I think more widely-read than myself, though one or two arguably more knowledgeable about some of the more obscure of the Jacobean philatelists.

I find myself in agreement with Socrates, whom I never knew personally, when he commends a proper reading programme as worthy of any young man's attention. My distinguished 15th century forebear, Henry Moog of Kidderminster, was an inveterate reader. Having been appointed Director-General of the Kidderminster Chamber of Commerce in 1476, a post he was later to pass on to his grandson, Henry Ross-Mugg of Kidderminster, he came to realise that life was like an enamel tea-cup, chipped in parts, but still useful, most particularly for the sipping of tea. Such knowledge as he had — and I suspect my own knowledge surpasses his in virtually every respect — was gained through reading the works of our joint 12th century ancestor, St Hilary of Mog Hill. St Hilary counselled against the vanities of this world. "'The truly learned man," she once wrote, "hath no need to boast of his learning." Words of wisdom, indeed, and echoed, I might add, in my recent re-reading of the complete works of Livy, Pliny, Silly and Libby (Purves) and also in the conversations I have granted every post-war Prime Minister (few of them first-rate, incidentally, but one or two perfectly sound).

In preparation for my new role as Chairman of the Broadcasting Standards Council, I put aside a very great deal of time to re-reading Plato, the Pentateuch and Mayhew, with more contemporary studies such as *Playboy*,

Penthouse and *Mayfair* also proving exceptionally informative. I now spend a large part of each day watching the "television", an occupation of which I had never availed myself before.

I must confess that for the first three months I couldn't see the fascination it held for so many millions of one's fellow Britons. It seemed to me a very dull affair: an utterly grey square, roughly two foot by two foot, fronted by a panel of glass. After many days staring at this blank "television", I began to realise that life itself might be an utterly grey square, fronted by a panel of glass, to be gazed at in search of useful meaning.

After three months, I was interrupted from my contemplations when a technician put his head around the door. "But the set's not on, squire," he commented. He then fiddled with a knob at the front. To my astonishment, a variety of moving pictures suddenly came onto the screen, and sound emerged from nowhere! It was now, I was informed, "switched on". As Chairman of the Broadcasting Standards Council, I now watch these moving pictures day after day. I conclude that we ignore the progress of science at our peril. My favourite programme? *Upstairs Downstairs*, a vivid portrait of day-to-day life in contemporary England.

TIM RICE

Came up with a truly smasherooni lyric at Easter. It's just a germ at the mo, but I'm hopping that — whoops — there goes my spelling! — smack-botty-time, Timothy! — I'm sorry, I'll say that again! — I'm *hoping* that the germ'll spread into a truly brill musical all about what happened on that first amazing Easter, literally years ago, somewhere incredibly abroad. To me, that first Easter is basically just one helluva great story, when the very first great big Easter Egg was opened, and everyone went absolutely wild and pigged out in no uncertain fashion on all the choccie and the sweeties inside and the first Easter bunny hop-hop-hopped around to the delight of all children everywhere.

For all the Rice buffs among you, the aforesaid germ's called 'Easter Egg!', or 'Egg!' for short, the tune's a bit like the one for 'Superstar!' and the lyrics go something like this:

Easter Egg!
Easter Egg!
Easter Egg!
Easter Egg!
Do you think your name is really Reg?
So far, the germ's not completely full blown, but with some instrumental work and maybe some totally amazing sets and a bit of a dinky overture I have high hopes we can make it spread to the full three hours. And the great news is that Elaine Paige has said she's very, very interested. Methinks it should be TT — or Totally Triff!

Like many artistes in the music biz, though I may seem to the rest of you to be a bit of a groover, I have a serious, more reflective side to my character. In fact, my enemies might accuse me of being pretty thoughtful at times. And that's why I support John Major and the Conservative Party and all they're trying to do on behalf of us all both in Europe and abroad. Luckily, the Prime Minister and I are both fully paid up cricket nuts, never happier than when zonking around with bat and ball! Anyway, the smashing news is that John — great bloke, nice sense of humour — has asked me to write a lyric for the Conservatives to help them slaughter the socialists at the next election. So far, I've just about got the first two lines fully polished—

Major!

Is all the rage. Er.

— and once I've got a rhyme for 'quite happily married to Norma' it'll be in the can, as the rest is mainly fanfares and trumpet voluntaries. Incidentally, Andy Lloyd Webber's knocking off the music, which should finally put paid to those who maintain there's some sort of 'rift' between us. Baloney: if Andrew wants to churn out universally successful money-making smash hit musicals, then good luck to him, and I admire the single-minded way he's always been absolutely determined to get exactly what he wants come what may, but frankly that's not my bag, I'd much rather devote my life to less obvious cult musicals with much shorter, more exclusive runs, well away from the money men of Broadway. Andrew's a terrific guy and I wish him all the luck in the world. If that's what he wants. Cheers!

Latest truly groovy proj is getting Cliff to star as Heathcliff in a musical based on the totally haunting Jane Austen novel of the same name. Take it from me. In some amazing way Cliff just completely *becomes* Heathcliff, so that I honestly guess that future generations will come to think of Heathcliff as this extraordinary guy in blue satin flares, a bright red cravat, beautiful lapels and a beautiful gold medallion, singing his heart out to the most memorabelissimo lyrics by — you guessed it! — yours truly:

I'm Heathcliff
I hardly ever sniff
Anybody here seen Cathy?
Talk about daffy!
Just nipping out to the lavvy
So keep ca-ve
'Cos my hair's all wavey
Gotta play that riff!
'Cos they call me Heath
Though my first name's Cliff!

Chorus: *Catherine! Catherine! Catherine! Did you take a bit of a batterin'?*

If that doesn't knock 'em for six, nothing will. By the way-zi-o, if any of you swingers out there are dreaming that you, too, might one day be able to earn a decent crust at the old lyric game, might I just draw your attention to an important but highly complex point? If you look at the last word of each line — 'Cathy', 'daffy', 'lavvy', 'ca-ve' and 'wavey' — you will note something totally unexpected and brilliant about 'em: they all *rhyme*. Most people probably think the job of a lyricist is as easy as falling off the proverbial wall, but this goes to show the amazing technical sleight-of-hand and sheer bloody craft needed to produce a truly memorable lyric. While we're on the old subjectio, not many people know that 'lyric' is an anagram of 'cyril'. Sorry! — I'm an absolute fund of such useless — but highly entertaining — information!!

It's a well-known fact that I've been the numero uno fan of rock 'n' roll — in my book the greatest art form ever invented by man since I first heard the immortal Bill Haley utterly knock my brains out with that awe-inspiring work of genius, 'See You Later, Alligator'. Frankly, what the big T.R. (that's me, folks!) doesn't know about rock music isn't worth writing on the back of a postage stamp.

I'm not saying I'm more intelligent than anyone else, but it sometimes surprises me that supposedly "clever" blokes get by with so little true knowledge. F'r'instance, I bumped into a geezer by the name of Dr Jonathan Miller the other day. Brainy? That's what people say. But after first establishing — to my considerable disappointment — that he wasn't related to Frankie Miller, Roger Miller, Steve Miller, Glenn Miller, or even Gary 'Yellow Rose of Texas' Miller, I set about testing that so-called intelligence.

"Okay, Jonathan," I said. "Which British singer had two number sevens in sixty three followed by a number nine and a number six in sixty four nothing at all in sixty five and then two successive number ones in sixty six before dropping to thirty three in sixty seven and then waiting five long years before charting at twenty one in seventy two?"

Honestly, I'm not kidding when I tell you he didn't have the foggiest. So I bowled him another, this time a complete dolly. "Which five piece band achieved three number ones in eighty three staying in the charts for forty six weeks then returned as a three piece or trio to record a song originally made famous by a seven-piece in fifty nine rising to number six in eighty seven?" Not a clue!

At that point I vamoosed PDQ, 'cos I was worried he wouldn't even know which major recording artiste climbed to number seven in ninety one before dropping to twelve in ninety two — a full eleven years after reaching number nineteen in eighty one. Some blokes!

ANITA RODDICK

I want to save the world. I'm sorry, but I do. When people the length and breadth of the globe talk endlessly about me and my extraordinary 'Body Shop' vision — and, my god, sometimes I wish they'd talk about something else for a change ! — they never cease to wonder at the full extent of my amazing love for this great planet of ours.

C'mon, they say — surely business is all about profit? No, I reply. It's about one helluva lot more than that.

● It's about distributing our *Honey and Oatmeal Scrub Mask (£6.75)* to the Yanamona rain-forest tribe of Brazil.

● It's about making damned sure that whales, porpoises, dolphins and hundreds of other endangered seafaring mammals are given the fullest possible access to our *Lettuce and Avocado Facial Wash (£4.50).*

● It's about encouraging local communities in Third World countries to utilise their resources to preserve their ancient tribal way of life through constant daily use of our *Peppermint and Strawberry Foot Lotion (£8.95).* That's the Body Shop dream, and it's a dream we want you, the customer, to share.

What I honestly can't understand is why so many people think I'm so marvellous. Here's a big admission — *most of my ideas aren't my own.* No — they're borrowed from some great people who shared my vision but for whatever reason couldn't put it into practice. Lovely, caring, *euphoric* people. People like Mahatma Gandhi, Dr Martin Luther King, Albert Einstein, Ludwig Wittgenstein, Pablo Picasso. Yes, these are the true brains behind The Body Shop and, without their intellectual support, I doubt I would ever have succeeded in quite the same way. And that's why it is now our company policy to pay tribute to each of these great figures on selected products in some of the most underprivileged parts of the world. At the moment, our *Dr Martin Luther King Seaweed and Muesli Shampoo and Ankle Rub (£5.50)* is selling magnificently in Ghana, while our *Albert Einstein Cucumber and Butterscotch Hair Gel (£6.75)* is going great guns in Peru. It's my own small way of saying Thanks, Albert and Martin. Thanks for the Dream.

I suppose I could be accused of being a bit of an idealist. It's so important to my whole intricate value-system that we campaign to preserve all the different ancient cultures of our planet, not letting them get washed away by the over-powering multi-nationals hell-bent on homogenising the world in pursuit of a quick buck. Frankly, it's a message I've been singing from the rooftops of over six hundred Body Shops worldwide. Come and hear the message at your local Body Shop. You can't fail to miss it — from Rio to Rejkavik, all our outlets are painted the same Body Shop green, have the same Body Shop logo and sell all the same Body Shop products in the same refillable Body Shop bottles. With the world currently all at sixes and sevens, it's nice to know The Body Shop is always the same, wherever in the world you may be.

You know, sometimes it makes me laugh to think that here am I, Anita Roddick, just another lovely, soppy old hippy with frizzy hair whose clothes are more often than not a shambles and who regards the world as her family and who brings tremendous love and vivacity to everything she puts her mind to — here am I, the same old Anita, saving the planet from future destruction. Back in 1976, when I opened my first Body Shop, frankly who'd have thought it?

Unlike more conventional businesspersons, I welcome lively discussion and argument from all our resourceful Body Shop staff. I like to drop in on each branch from time to time — just wearing my usual T-shirt and jeans, that's the kind of person I am — and we gather in a circle and then they confront me totally frankly with any complaints and suggestions they might have. They know I welcome criticism, and so they're not afraid to give it — however uncomfortable it might be for me! Believe it or not, they have one recurring complaint, but I'm big enough to take it. "Lovely Anita," they say. "Why the heck don't you take more credit for saving the world? It's simply not fair that you receive so little publicity for the extraordinary work you've done repairing the ozone layer, stopping acid rain and calling a halt to the rain forests! You're a super person, Anita — but we do wish you were more assertive."

Point Taken. But frankly I've always cared more for promoting my vision than for promoting myself. And that's why my current T-shirt campaign:

"Recycle the Tibetan whale"
SAYS ANITA RODDICK
OF BODY SHOP

carries the slogan first, and me — Anita Roddick of Body Shop — only second. That way, the real message gets over, loud and clear.

My critics have sometimes attacked me for being a brilliant revolutionary determined to inject my unique personal warmth into the cynical world of big business. I know full well that some of my rivals complain that without any formal business training I have managed to transform the heartless world of big business into a force for love and idealism.

Certainly, I have tried to make The Body Shop not just another brilliantly successful high street store but a centre of education for the propagation of environmental and social ideals. But I would argue that our customers in all our six hundred shops in thirty-seven different countries all love us for it, queuing up for our *Spearmint and Kennomeat Ozone-Free Nose Rub (£4.25)* or our *Wholemeal Pasta and Cream of Tomato Soup Back Rub and Brain Softener (£5.95)*, knowing that, by doing so, they are managing to do their bit to Free Nelson Mandela.

These last few weeks have been terrible for the war-torn people of Sarajevo. Frankly, I admire their guts — and this tribute from a mere woman who, way back in 1976, showed the sheer guts to start the very first Body Shop in Brighton on a shoe-string budget and with a staff of just one (me!). But we in the Body Shop — now over 600 branches strong — don't like to sit idly by. With our customers' help, we're determined to organise a special Body Shop airlift of much-needed supplies to that tragic city. And this is where you, the customer, come in. The poor people of Sarajevo are literally crying out for the following:

● *15,000 bots. Glycerine and Dried Yam Skin Toner (£5.95 each)*
● *19,500 bots. Salt and Vinegar Body-Tuning Massage Cream (£4.25,)*
● *32,000 Emergency Prune and Baked Bean Knee-Rub Kits (£5.50)*
● *17,000 bots. 100% Recycled Waste Skincare Syrup (£6.25)*

Come on, save the World. Give us the Money. Love ya! Anita.

KEN RUSSELL

Creative? My God — My Hitler! My Nymphomaniac Nun! — I'm creative, you bet I am! My whole body tingles with wild, free, exciting — *controversial!* — artistic vision morning, noon and night. Let me stab you through the eyes with an example. This morning, I was all set to brush my teeth, but just as I was squeezing the tube and the toothpaste was oozing out, I thought, My God, it's like Rimsky-Korsakov's penis! You see, that's the way my amazing, brilliant — *and sometimes controversial!* — mind works, it's just so full of extraordinary visions and weird insights you just simply wouldn't believe it!

Of course, the genuine artist in our society has never been understood in his lifetime, and that's why my film of *Lady Chatterley* is arousing such a vindictive, hate-filled response from the bastard (does that shock you? does it? well, I'll repeat it then: *bastard!*) critics. Well, if that puts me in a line with Van Gogh (Phil Collins), Mozart (Roger Tonge) and Liszt (Roger Daltrey) then so be it, I'm delighted I can add my extra lustre to their reputations. If people can't understand me, then that's a price worth paying for being one of the world's great visionaries — and you know, sometimes I can't even understand myself, my mind's so endlessly inventive, so soaked by the semen of creativity!

At the moment, I'm composing my next project, a screen version of The Life of James Last, the brilliant — *controversial!* — and hopelessly misunderstood Scandinavian orchestral leader who lived for his music as no other man had ever done and sweated blood to conjure up his own mad and incredible vision of things. I've called it *controversially!* — *Lastomania!* and it opens on the Golden Gate Bridge, transposed to the Swiss Fjords, where James Last played by Oliver Reed — is practising frantically with his baton as the rain thunders down in loud guitar-bursts:

Mrs Last: Oh James, James, James! Have you not suffered enough? Must you always live for music! music! music! and nothing else? Let us to bed!

(Mrs Last removes her leather one-piece costume decked out in swastikas. Beneath it is another leather one-piece costume decked out in swastikas)

Mrs Last: Take me, maestro!

James Last *(pulling out a thirty-foot high phallic symbol dousing it with petrol and setting fire to it)*: Not now, dear! Before the dawn cometh, I must, must, must finish my new work, "Non-Stop-Party-Hits-A-Go-Go Volume 10" or my very creative juices will fail me and I will shrivel to nothing! Art is torture!

Mrs Last: Your music is a hymn to nature, sure enough, James Last. But what about me? Do I not have my own needs and desires, husband? You may have conquered the world of easy listening, James — but still you cannot conquer your own wife!

(Mrs Last erupts in a mad cackle. She ships off and dives naked into the Fjord, which becomes awash with the bodies of dead nuns. Choking on her own vomit, she struggles desperately and drowns. The stirring soundtrack is — poignantly — Last's own version of 'Would You Like To Fly (In My Beautiful Balloon)?')

James Last: Did you say something, dear? You see, like many mad and crazy artists, I sometimes become so involved in the act of creation that I am prone to neglect those around me. But at least the new album will be arranged by tomorrow, and that's the main thing, eh dear? Dear? Dear? *(Suddenly he realises that his wife is floating face down beneath the bodies of dead nuns)* Oh my God! What have I done for my art?

Not a bad scene-setter, eh? By a series of subtle hints and juxtapositions, with here a clever metaphor and there a suggestive symbol, I introduce the viewer to the massive torments and contradictions in the paradoxical character of James Last — his passionate love of music coupled with his inability to reach out beyond fantasy into a darker reality. By the end of the first scene, he has composed his next album, his wife has drowned and his penis has been set on fire. And then things really start happening. Incidentally, we're hoping to get that superb young actress Hetty Baines to play Mrs Last — fingers crossed!

My wife — that superb young actress Hetty Baines — tells me I'm a bit of an *enfant terrible*. I'm certainly not denying that I'm not frightened to shock. All great artists have felt the need to shock their public into seeing the world with fresh and terrified eyes. Why else would Constable paint a field of dildoes to the left of Flatford Mill (see my acclaimed biopic *"Constable!"* (1973)). And why else would Sir Edward Elgar have written his celebrated *"Cello Concerto for Nuns and Nazis"*? (*"IncredibElgar!"* (1984)) And why else would Virginia Woolf have smeared herself in lard and danced naked in Nazi jackboots on the top of the Eiffel Tower? (*"Woolfomania!"* (1991)) Shocking? Well, perhaps life and art — and genius — are all shocking. But apologise for my genius before a drab, grey, philistine world? Sorry: no can do. I'd rather die in poverty, skeletal, starving, and diseased, rejected by an unthinking world that doesn't understand me, faithful to the very end to the vision of my genius, just like Shakespeare did.

After *Lastomania!* (see above), I'm embarking on a strikingly new four-part production for BBC/TV called *Janie!*, a film-portrait of Jane Austen. I aim to explore the side of her character that has long been unduly neglected, the side of her character that was sex-crazed and sado-masochistic and obsessed with firearms, leather gear, whips, fire and fast cars.

The first episode opens with the young Jane — played, if we can get her, by that superb young actress, Hetty Baines — clad only in her famous rubber bikini, driving up to Hitler's Berlin bunker in her Austin (witty touch) before mass-murdering over five hundred nuns to the tune of "Edelweiss". This will go a long way, I think, towards unlocking the secret of the artistic genius who wrote such undoubted masterpieces as *Emma!*, *Rebecca!*, and *Wuthering Heights!* Ken Russell gets it together with Jane Austen — that sounds to me like a terrific recipe for art, for passion, and — let's face it — for maybe just a smidgin of ***controversy!!!***

FRIENDS OF SALMAN

Salman, old buddy, old chum, I have thought of you often over the last few years: of how your own persecution for what you believe in is so like my own. The writer's life is one of paranoia and mayhem, dammit, and I guess that's the price we pay. You know, Salman, my old prize-fighter, when I think of you, I think of my own arm-wrestling with the daemons of governments and of my struggle in that most ungovernable and terrifying terrain — the imagination — and of how I overcame both these forces through sheer bloody spunk and sweat. Shucks, some people didn't know just how tough it was to be a writer before you and I came along, Salman, old bean. Now, looking at you, they can have a fresh understanding of writers like me. Brave it out, old trout, and when you finally emerge from your solitary martyrdom, I'm gonna straightaway place my new book — 1500 pages on the Jansenist heresy set in Ancient Greece, told by a dyslexic castrato, half in Esperanto, half in Catalan — in those world-weary yet hopeful hands of yours. And as I watch you read it word by word, from cover to cover, I know I'll be witnessing a man tasting his joyous sips of true freedom. So my best to you, old pardner, wherever you are ensconced, and may my muses embrace you.

Norman Mailer

Dear Salman, To me, you're more than a man called Sal, because what you Sell Man is something indeed to Rush and Die for. You uphold the *beacon* of hope because where you are holed-up no *bee can* hop. You have introduced the word *fatwa* into our language, and a *fatwa* lot of good it's done us. I think of you shooed into solitude, just as the mischievous dog thinks of his master's shoe and the sole-'e-chewed. Like the best of us, you have suffered for your art: how much easier it would be if we could have (p)arted with our supper.

Yours sincerely, because you are so sincerely you,

Clive James

Remember, Salman, how we were once sitting together talking about literature, its magic, its ability to transform our world into something *other*, and how marvellous life was, and love was, and I was, and how you said to me, "I love your new play, Arnold, and I advise everyone out there to go and see it — it's without doubt a modern masterpiece, and much better than anything I could've written myself"? Perhaps you don't. Perhaps you'll say you never met me — but too bad, you can't answer back, that's the awful thing about this fatwa! News from the real world must be more important than ever to you now, Salman, shut away as you are. So I know you'll want to know that I am speaking at various prestigious Literature Festivals throughout the North of England in the next few months. Do drop by if you're in the area: I'd dearly love to share all my latest ideas with you.

Arnold Wesker

Dearest Salman, Though I have never met you, I feel you know me.

You are the outcast. So am I. For I am a high-earning divorced woman novelist. A quadruple paradox. And it makes me hated and shunned by our society. If they could kill me, they would. Yet you have men day-and-night guarding you, and I am all alone in our urban wilderness. Such is the lot of woman.

Can I offer some advice to help you get through your ordeal? It's advice women like me have to take every single day of our lives. For we are prisoners like you.

Go out and get your hair done. It can make you feel a million dollars.

Curl up in bed with a super book and a nice box of choccies. Lovely.

Listen to some of your favourite music on the gramophone and sing along at the top of your voice.

Phone an old friend for a jolly good gossip.

And remember, Salman: life is a peanut. Sometimes ready salted, and sometimes not. Sometimes in a bag. And sometimes already laid out on a dish. But always there to nibble if you're feeling frightfully naughty.

With warmest regards. Think of me.

Fay Weldon

My Dear Salman, As you are only too well aware I have been unashamedly unequivocal in my support for you during this least efficacious of ordeals, whilst nevertheless being profoundly mindful of the very great hurt you have caused a number of my very good friends in the Asian community — ordinary, decent citizens for whom the taking of another life though wholly repugnant under normal conditions would, within this context, be profoundly understandable.

I always maintain that it is the hallmark of the fully-paid-up member of the human race that the luxury of persecution must be paid for with a sense of remorse on the part of the persecuted.

Let us not for one moment beat around the clump of shrubs containing stems of moderate length. Those of us who have assuaged our hard-pressed bank-managers by earning a nutritious crust from our collected jottings have a duty to those who have never enjoyed the pleasures of verbiage to respect their higher feelings. A solitary life under threat of death seems to me inadequate remuneration for indignities heaped on an oppressed minority by any highly-paid author. As you are aware, Salman, you have my absolute support; however, if you should so decide — of your own volition, let me hasten to add! — to surrender your person to the goodly burghers of Iran, then that would be not only a courageous gesture but a courteous response to a very real problem.

Yours in the struggle for free speech (with responsibility),

Roy Hattersley

MARTIN SCORSESE

Am I religious? Religious? Am I? Am I religious? Huh? I am religious. You remember the scene in *Taxi Driver* when De Niro pumps Keitel in the head with the shotgun? You remember? And a trickle of blood comes out his nose?

That trickle of blood is a rosary.

The whole scene — the massacre of the pimps and the gun-runners by De Niro, who's a kind of avenging angel — has always reminded me of Piero della Francesca's *Madonna della Misericordia*, it has the same kind of deep spiritual quality. I get a lot of inspiration from Renaissance painters, you know. It looks like my next movie might be *The Sistine Chapel Ceiling* reset in the Bronx with guns and one hell of a lot of anger: Adam's always pointing the finger at God and God says who is this guy anyway and why can't he quit buggin' me huh? and God can't take it no more and he's out for *revenge*. It's my own, very personal reaction to the Bible story, and I see no reason why it should cause offence.

All my films are about religion and morality, how a good man should behave in the modern world. Take this scene from my movie *Bastard Bunny Kill* (1973), my re-working of the Beatrix Potter stories set in urban New York with De Niro as Peter Rabbit:

(Cut to)

Peter Rabbit: Huh?

(Close up)

Farmer MacGregor: *(The Black Pimp)*: Jeez…

(Rabbit's hand moves to shoulder holster)

MacGregor: Shit man…

(Rabbit pumps MacGregor twelve times through head)

MacGregor: Jeez…

Rabbit: Huh?

MacGregor: Shit man…

Rabbit: Huh?

MacGregor: Ugh.

(Mrs Tiggywinkle enters room naked. She bristles)

Rabbit: Huh?

Tiggywinkle: Jeez.

(Rabbit throttles Tiggywinkle with bare hands, finishes her off with pump-action shotgun)

Tiggywinkle: Shit man…

Rabbit: Huh?

(Close up, Peter Rabbit in confessional)

Everytime I see that scene, I'm totally moved by it. It's like the Crucifixion. The hedgehog is the crown of thorns, only they're now saying the historical Jesus didn't wear a hedgehog, just a crown of thorns, I don't know, maybe a hedgehog would have over-run his budget.

In *Bastard Bunny Kill*, De Niro was dead set on playing the rabbit just right so he spent four months pacing himself for the role by eating carrots, hanging around kitchen gardens and growing his ears. Jeez, the guy's a perfectionist.

He becomes every role he plays — the angry loner in *Cape Fear*, or the loner who's kinda angry in *Taxi Driver*, or the lonely, angry guy in *Mean Streets* or the really angry loner in *King of Comedy* or the angry guy who's kinda lonely in *Cape Fear*. And he can bring so much to a role. Originally, I wanted him to play Christ in my movie *The Last Temptation of Christ*.

"Howdya see it, Bob, huh? The role of Christ, Bob, howdya see it, huh?" I asked him.

I watched him as he thought long and hard. Then he looked me straight in the face and he said, "Marty," he said, "Marty, the guy's a loner. And he's angry, huh?"

"Jeez, Bob," I said, "That's uncanny! That's just the way I see him too, huh! Let's make it together, Bob!" But in the end Bob was booked for another project, playing the part of the angry loner in the remake of *Dr Doolittle*, so I got some other guy for Jesus, and that guy brought his own interpretation to the role, playing him as more of an angry loner.

From my earliest days, I've always been in love with cinema. It has occupied all my care and attention from as far back as I can remember. My quest for beauty in the cinema is never-ending. Like, when I was filming *Raging Bull*, about this lonely guy, full of anger — a role played, after many months of sitting in a gym being punched by one of my favourite actors, Bob De Niro — I wanted to capture the real beauty of Jake La Motta having his nose punched outta shape.

Again and again, I referred back to Italian masterpieces such as Caravaggio's *Death of the Virgin* and Giorgione's *Tempest*. Again and again, I would re-run scenes from great old movies such as *The Bicycle Thieves* and *Citizen Kane* to see if they contained angry loners being punched senseless. Then, for forty days and forty nights, our ninety-strong crew stayed in that boxing ring. We miked up Bob's gloves and his nose and for this sequence I even strapped the camera to his chest, so you go with the hit. In the movie, the scene lasts just five seconds — you see the glove coming — cut to the nose — then to the glove — then fist hits nose — cut to blood spurting out, like in a Canaletto fountain.

Then Bob has the line "Uh". Simple but beautiful, but Bob had to get to know every damn part of his character before he could get to grips with that line. He said to me, he said, "Marty, what does a guy actually *feel* when he has his nose punched? What do you think he's *going through*?"

"Bob," I said after a lot of thought, "Bob I'd guess he feels kinda — how'd you put it? — beat up." So we settled that Bob would say "Uh" with a kinda hurt, kinda beat-up expression angry, yeah, lonely, yeah — but also kinda, well, beat-up.

So we filmed for a month, never quite getting the beat-up expression I was after. That "Uh" just didn't sound beat-up enough. So eventually I pulled Bob to one side, set the cameras going and punched him with great force in the nose. "UH!" he said, "UH!" — giving us a choice of two perfect UHs for the final cut. "Jeez, Bob," I said, "You're so instinctive."

It causes me a hell of a lot of pain when my movies are misunderstood by the world at large. For instance, they say they're violent. Huh! It's my opinion that they are fiercely moral tales, born of my deep sense of inner conflict with Catholicism, parables against violence and revenge in our sick society. Like, in that scene in *Stabbing Strangers* (1975) where Rick, the angry loner, oppressed by Catholic guilt and a sense of deep moral duty, hacks the head off his girlfriend Karen before stabbing to death his best friend Steve — I wanted to show that no good comes of violence, so that when Rick tries to do the same thing again the next day, he finds it's no good, Steve is already dead and Karen has already had her head hacked off and so he realised you can't kill the same man twice, you have to pick on someone new. As I read it, this is the stark message of Jesus Christ in the New Testament. So why do people say I got violence on the brain, huh? They need their heads examined. Or better still shot to pieces with an automatic pump-action shotgun, huh?

BRIAN SEWELL

A brisk coastal walk in the midst of the historic English countryside on a sunlit day does much to expose the repellent inanities of the Creator. Hills and hillocks, predictable beyond endurance, regurgitate their irksome bumpiness as far as the eye can see; grass, bladish, modishly vertiginous and tiresomely damp, seemingly unashamed to be coloured such a preposterously vivid and idiotic green, spreads itself far and wide over mountain and valley, like the venereal disease of a poxy tart. And what, may one be excused for asking, lies beneath this conceited assortment of rural rubbish? The answer is dirt, dirt and more dirt, grubby beyond endurance, ready to soil one's fingernails if ever one were to exhibit the generosity to allow them, unvarnished, within its vicinity. The sense of symmetry and balance in the countryside is execrable too. Trees, "shrubs" and wild flowers popping up any-old-how, and the hopelessly over-rated sea, much beloved of the pusillanimous panjandrums of the Arts Council and such weary old deadbeats as the dauber Turner, is merely noisy, brash, tediously repetitive, incoherent in its splutterings and vulgarly moist. Overall, there is no evidence whatsoever to suggest that anything higher than a fifth-rate mind has been at work, slipshod and vapid, entertaining itself with flimsy doodles more expertly executed by a blind lesbian black spinster pupil at a fortnight's summer school in Little Piddlehinton. Few contemporary critics possess the moral probity to voice such honest opinions about these wretchedly scruffy shibboleths of our lacklustre age. I daresay I tell an uncomfortable truth, but mine is a voice that shall not be stifled, even by the Stalins and Hitlers who now wield their monstrous power in the boardrooms of the Royal Academy and the Tate, and who desire abject subservience from all scribblers. Bah!

It is incumbent upon the trained art historian to note, with a dismal drooping of the heart, that all artists from the year dot have proved deeply disappointing, alas without exception. Even the so-called "major" artists are, it pains me most dreadfully to say, gravely flawed, each one of them lacking that essential ingredient that makes for true art. Monet, for all his pretty colouring, never so much as bothered to tackle a cow or any other farmyard animal, even though the countryside around Givenchy must have been teeming with them. Vermeer simply didn't have the energy, the vision or the guts to paint a group portrait. Far too many of Rembrandt's later paintings are just self, self, self, and he was wilfully blind to the merits of mauve and pink, preferring the odious, jumped-up sewagey brown. Velasquez, for all his overweening self-confidence, couldn't paint a still-life for toffee; indeed, he never even tried. Cezanne never had the nerve to risk his reputation and paint a single cat, Goya pooh-poohed the English countryside and, of course, the arrival of the Industrial Revolution is totally ignored by the artists of the Renaissance, who preferred, in their finickety, gesticulative Italian way, to contemplate the navels of themselves and others. If only one or two of them had possessed the breadth of reference, the intellectual passion, the iron discipline, the baroque gusto, the unashamed genius of, say, a properly trained, all-seeing art historian with a weekly column in a London evening newspaper — why, what marvels they might have produced!

The sight, preposterous and grotesque, of a naked woman, glimpsed briefly but no less horrifyingly in a late-night televisual cinematogram, has filled me, as it would fill any other scrupulous critic, if any there be, and there be not, with a despair bordering on profound and abject depression.

This most distressing of events occurred the night before last. The woman so glimpsed was young — a pert twentyish — and, would, no doubt, be regarded by the rag-tag and bobtail of mawkish, sheeplike, tiresomely malleable, mankind as somehow "attractive". Yet the keener eye of the trained art historian could detect two cumbersome, squishy-squashy lumps on her chest area, each with a singularly poorly placed "nipple" the size of an old pennypiece or an ill-fitting bathroom plug. And where, may one ask, was her penis? In any reasonable society, this personable and historic appendage would be regarded as the very *sine qua non* of physical probity. Yet it was nowhere to be seen!

"Faulty model. Take it back" would be the natural reaction of anyone with a tuppenny-halfpenny'orth of sense, but the eximious panjandrums,pompous poseurs, self-congratulatory nincompoops, verbose nitwits and hopelessly faddy *cacafuegos* of the contemporary art world conspire to teach us otherwise, forcing their half-baked populist puerilities onto those institutions — insTITutions, one almost might say, a touch mischievously(!) — over which they so ploddingly preside, dictatorially determined to show that even if WE do not like the look of these skew-whiff creatures, these wonky women, then they most certainly do, so boo-snubs to the rest of us.

Thus we are treated to the preposterous situation in which perfectly monstrous women of every hue, ache, mould and scratching are riding roughshod through even our most sacred portals; women as critics, women as curators, women as models, women as art historians and now women as *artists*, forsooth! Fie on you, say I! Begone, brazen hussies! Take your shrill warblings, your beskirted doodlings, your incongruous, flippy-floppy boobies elsewhere!

Fig (a):

This is not what I would describe as a line, straight or otherwise. Far from it; any fourth-form student (preferably male) would be able to explain that it is merely a lazy and self-serving *cacafuego* or an extended dot, needlessly and odiously prolonged between two points, a contemptibly elongated affront to the past glories of Western civilisation, rousing the stomach, not to mention the *derrière*, to objection.

Many claims have been made by the incompetent and fraudulent bores of the London Arts mafia for this singularly commonplace blob (fig b), the most preposterous being that it is in some apparently indefinable sense a "circle". As a trained art historian, it seems to me not unreasonable to point out that it is nothing of the kind, but merely a straight line masquerading as a circle, employing the tired old trick of rolling back on itself in order to promote the illusion of circularity. I suppose this might guarantee it a place on *The Late Show* or the ineffable *Kaleidoscope*, but I hereby aver that no serious historian would give it the time of day, pshaw.

Fig (b):

GODFREY SMITH

A plump mailbag this week, chums. The quest for the world's most utterly worthless column-filler thunders on. Cheers and thanks aplenty to Mr Charles Smethwick from Tring, Herts, who writes: "Why not, prithee, a few rich tales of our old mate Kipling, Rudyard of that ilk? Two or three of 'em, and you'd have the column filled in no time, much to the pleasure of the Island Race!"

Cracking suggestion, Charlie, for Kippers is indeed a name with which to conjure. I was reminded of this by mates aplenty at the annual chin-wag and tuck-in of The Kipling Society on Tuesday last. Over some first-class nosh, we heard from Professor Geoffrey Leakey of Balliol that 'The Kip' was an inveterate wearer of sensible shoes. "He never went outside without 'em!" the Good Prof informed us over a first-class Port.

I approached Geoffrey after dinner and asked him to explain the vexed mystery of why Kipling was so insistent on quality footwear. "I can only think that it was so that his feet wouldn't get wet!" answered Geoff. Sometimes, it seems, the simplest explanations are also the truest! I hope that clears the matter up for you, Mr C.! Do any other readers wear shoes, perchance — or is it another tradition that is going the way of the penny-farthing and the good old-fashioned rolypoly?

"Is there a God?" asks reader Mr Arnold Petty from Yorks. Well, Mr P., there's a puzzler! You're not the first person who's asked that particular brain-teaser, and I feel sure you won't be the last, but, anyway, here goes!

Yes, Arnie, on balance I'd say there was a God — if only because I've always hoped that there's someone larger than me in this Universe of ours. But others of Our Island Race have felt rather differently, of that there's no denying. That inveterate egghead Bertrand Russell was of the sage opinion that there wasn't a God, and after much to-ing and fro-ing, our old friend Sigmund Freud found himself agreeing with Bertie.

But God has been able to muster quite a line-up of supporters for Himself, from our very own Archbish. of C., to that most popular of Poles, Il Papa! They all insist he's a first-class bloke, and a true gent to boot. This is one debate that looks to rage on for some months yet. A magnum of the fizzy stuff will be wending its way to the reader who comes up with the best answer. Let's be hearing from you!

My dictionary definition of the word 'buzzer' says, 'an electrical device, similar to a bell, that makes a buzzing noise'. Just above it, the entry for 'buzzard' reads, 'any of a group of predatory birds of the hawk family, esp. of the genus *butea*, with broad wings well adapted for soaring flight'.

Fascinating what one can find in one's trusty dictionary, particularly if one's short of something to fill the old column! And, as friend Einstein may well have once observed, the dictionary can get one out of some pretty ticklish situations. For example, I'll know now never to mix up a buzzer with a buzzard thus saving the old forefinger from a pretty sharp nip from our feathered friend! A bottle of fizz for the reader who thinks of other uses to which a trusty dictionary may be put...

Bumped into my old chum Alexander Solzhenitsyn the other morn, or might have done had he been in town, and I'm delighted to report that he still has that truly magnificent beard for which he was once so famous.

It emerges that Sandy keeps his beard in trim with the occasional visit to his local barber, but otherwise, he says, it looks after itself. Of course, in the old days some of the best of the British Bards were fully-paid-up members of the hairy chin brigade, Tony Trollope, Benjy Disraeli and Charlie Dickens among'em. But now their numbers seem to be slipping, though my old chum Bill Golding is a notable exception — and a Nobel Prize-winner to boot!

Why the beard, Bill, old bean? Like me, Bill Golding is a devoted reader of this column, so I trust he'll drop me a line to set the record straight on this most hairy of questions. And a bottle of fizz, too, to the reader who comes up with the best ending to the following sentence — 'I think our chum Bill Golding, sports a beard because...' But please — no more than twelve words thank you. Over to you!

A Mr Philip Peters, who hails from Dorking, Surrey, writes a delightful letter. 'If you don't have anything else to fill up your column this week, Godders.' he says. 'then why not shove this letter in?'

Thanks, Phil, old chap — I most certainly will!

Thanks are also due to my inveterate correspondent Mr Malcolm Assington from the windswept metropolis of Torbay, who puts to me that perennial brain-teaser, 'What makes Britain Great'?

By heaven, that's surely one for the little grey cells, Malc! For me, the Great British Banger is something to sing about, and so too, I reckon, are good old Fish and Chips, the Queen Mum, Radio 4, Heinz Baked Beans, the Brussels Sprout and our unique ability to enjoy a damned good bellylaugh at our own expense!

And raise your glasses, if you will, to the Channel Tunnel. 'The *what?*' will be the response on the lips of most readers, so let me fill you in on this most delicious of developments, chums.

Last week at The Trollope Society Dinner, I found myself tucking into some scrumptuous scoff with a Mr Andrew Torrington, who it turned out, is a bigwig in the building of the Channel Tunnel. I'd never heard of the blessed thing me'self, so I begged Andy to tell me more, and fascinating stuff it proved to be.

Seems that for the last few years the blighters have been building a tunnel 'twixt Britain and France, the Brits busily burrowing from one end, the Frogs from t'other. Before many moons have passed, the intrepid traveller will thus be able to journey from London to Gay Paree without once setting foot on water! Sounds interesting!

Blimey! If that doesn't constitute a Great British achievement, then I'd like to know what does! Yes it was news to me, and to most of you too, I'll hazard. Trust the Island Race to keep such a smashing project under our collective hat for so long! Still, it's something to sing about in these dark times — and that can't be bad!

Finally, the usual bottle of the fizzy stuff to the reader who writes this column for me. Replies shouldn't be less than eight hundred words long — and I promise to print each one!
Cheers!

DR ROBIN SKYNNER AND JOHN CLEESE

John: Let me ask you something that has puzzled me a lot over the years. What do we mean when we say that someone is "a bit of a bore"?

Robin: I suppose, John, that on the deepest level we mean that he or she is going on and on about something quite "boring", something of interest only to themselves. And, of course, repeating himself.

John: "Repeating himself,"?

Robin: Repeating himself.

John: I see. So someone who "repeats himself" stands in danger of becoming "a bit of a bore".

Robin: Certainly. If he repeats himself, then —

John: He could become "a bit of a bore"?

Robin: Quite. If he repeats himself.

John: One thing I've always wanted to know, Robin, is why quite intelligent people — comedians and so forth — often like to talk in public about themselves all the time: their problems, their innermost thoughts, their feelings about themselves, and so on?

Robin: Good point, John. In layman's terms, this is what we call "talking about yourself in public", often to the exclusion of all others. Broadly speaking, the world can be divided up into two groups of people: people who always talk about themselves, and people who never talk about themselves. Research shows that though quite a few people always talk about themselves, and about the same number never talk about themselves, most of us are in a third group, somewhere in the middle, of people who occasionally talk about themselves, but certainly not all the time.

John: So what you're really saying, if I've understood you correctly, is that the vast majority of people occasionally talk about themselves, but certainly not all the time?

Robin: Correct.

John: Yes, I know what you mean. I used to talk about myself all the time — my "problems", my "innermost thoughts", my "feelings about myself', and so on — but, thanks to psychotherapy, I now find that I talk about myself in public only very occasionally —

Robin: And another thing worth mentioning is —

John: I'm sorry, if I could just finish, Robin — I was just saying that, speaking personally, I now find that psychotherapy has helped me "come to terms" with my past need to "talk about myself', and that I can now be much more objective, showing an interest in other people.

Robin: I —

John: Because, speaking personally for a second, I feel that I have somehow "got out of myself", and can now concentrate on spiritual, psychological and philosophical matters outside my own little world. "Me", if you like, is now less important than "You".

Robin: I —

John: But, forgive me, I'd like to hear what you have to say for a second! How would you describe me, for instance, to someone who had never met me?

John: What do we mean when we say we feel "happy"?

Robin: It's probably best described as feeling the opposite of "sad". Most people are "happy" some of the time and "sad" some of the time, but most of the time they feel something "in between".

John: Neither very happy nor very sad?

Robin: Quite so.

John: And what comes after the letter "D" in the "ABC"?

Robin: For most people, "E".

John: And then "F"?

Robin: Usually.

John: And is "E" a happy letter; or a sad one?

Robin: Probably somewhere in between.

John: I suppose that in many ways it's infantile and regressive to talk about letters as "happy" or "sad".

Robin: Certainly.

John: After all, they're only letters. They have their off-days like everybody else.

John: Why is it only married couples who divorce one another? Is there something about marriage which encourages divorce, do you think?

Robin: In the vast majority of cases, divorce comes about after married couples "fall out" with one another. But of course, if they had remained single, they would not then be in a position to get a divorce.

John: Or if they had never met one another in the first place?

Robin: Certainly.

John: So it follows that the two people — let's call them Person "A" and Person "B" — should never actually meet if they want to avoid the awful prospect of divorce?

Robin: They are certainly increasing their chances for a potential divorce in the years ahead if they first get to meet one another.

John: And what's the best way for "A" to avoid meeting "B"?

Robin: Well, if they live in different parts of the world, and in different socioeconomic groups, then that's half the battle won.

John: But surely they might still meet? On holiday, for instance.

Robin: Certainly, that's a risk.

John: So what's the best place to go on holiday in order to avoid meeting your future wife, and the whole thing ending in a distressing divorce, awful for the children and potentially ruinous to the inner psyche?

Robin: We're venturing into very difficult territory here, John. It's advisable to consult a qualified travel agent on this one, I think.

John: Quite.

John: Why are so many people these days so very "negative"? For instance, a lot of humour these days seems extremely cynical and "nonpositive". Shouldn't we be encouraging our young comedians to be more caring, healthy and "upfront"? It upsets me, for instance, that so few young comedians are writing books telling people how to enjoy better, richer, more fulfilled lifestyles. Instead, they're just telling jokes, often just for a laugh. To put it in a nutshell, what kind of world are we living in, Robin?

Robin: Surveys suggest that we're living in a world full of people of all nationalities inhabiting a variety of types of domicile in a great many different countries, John.

John: You mean there are literally millions of different people in the world, apart from me, of course?

Robin: At a rough approximation, yes, though I'm sticking my neck out a bit here.

John: So the expression, "it takes all sorts," first used by Gurdjieff — or was it Fromm — has a ring of truth to it?

Robin: In a nutshell, yes.

John: And what, in layman's terms, is a "nutshell"?

Robin: Broadly speaking, it's a shell containing a nut.

TAKI

I spotted my old buddy Hieronymous Bisto, of Bisto Gravy fame, in Harry's Bar last Tuesday. He was dining with Angelica Smedley, the fishcake millionairess, who happens to be a very old friend of the ex-wife of a close business associate of the daughter of Louis van Skunk III, the self-styled former American ambassador to Gstaad. Louis once played an heroic round of bridge with my old Vietnam veteran buddy Ritzi van Toewarmer, the international sock tycoon. I once enjoyed a spot of monkey business with his lissome daughter Gratuitee van Toewarmer. For some reason, like so many other women — ah, the fair sex! — she found this poor little Greek boy irresistibly attractive. Gratuitee was in a state of womanly tears when I told her later that day I was due to dine *à deux* with the fabulously attractive society hostess Brandi Mobile, the portable telephone heiress, whose former husband Prince Heinz von Trashcan, the scion of international refuse collectors, was also, as it happens, an old buddy of my old buddy Hieronymous Bisto, of Bisto Gravy fame. Small world, *n'est-ce pas?*

The problems of Northern Ireland are uppermost in people's minds, and so they should be: on a Saturday afternoon it is quite impossible to get from the hideous but hugely comfortable County Down mansion of my old friend the Hon Kitty Katt of pet-food fame to the rolling acres of Castle Ballyhoo, the far-from-unstately home of my old buddies Lord and Lady Floss, of the distinguished old dental hygiene family, without running into a traffic jam on the main Belfast to Antrim road. This means that guests of both households are often up to half an hour late for their respective meals, incurring the understandable displeasure of their delicious hosts. My old chum, the excellent Sir Paddy Mayhew — whose second cousin's home I once visited in the company of my old friend Jonathan Aitken OE, who once met Jackie Onassis — must give his fullest attention to an urgent solution to this Northern Ireland problem. Otherwise he may find that the province becomes beset with a handful of social troubles which could take many years to sort out.

Friends in high places tell me that my old friend Johnny Patten is likely to be replaced soon as Secretary of State for Education. Odds are that the job will go to my chum Nicholas Soames OE. Watch this space: your intrepid reporter will keep you posted.

I am, for my sins, well known as a wit. It is, my enemies tell me, as much for my skills as a raconteur as for my good looks not to mention my command of the English words that I am invited to all the very best homes in the Western hemisphere, including the luxury Costa del Sol Surrey-style maisonette of Wendy Burger,the international catering heiress, situated on the exclusive Rivermead estate overlooking the prestigious new Touristica development with panoramic sea views from the easily accessible roof. Last Friday, I found myself at dinner with seven Nobel prize-winners, one ex-President of the United States, three Oscar winners, two former Prime Ministers, three international financiers, four world famous authors and five European Heads of State. As you would expect, yours truly entertained them all to a splendid selection of anecdotes concerning the great and the frankly not-so-great, including a good crack against the loathsome nouveau Teddy Kennedy, who is well known to my good friends Baron and Baroness Thyssen Bornemisza, the Honourable Boofy Plunket-Earle-Greene OE, the Prince of Wales and Their Graces The Duke and

Duchess of Abercrombie as an incorrigible name-dropper, a disgusting foreigner, an inveterate womaniser and a deep-down hypocrite to boot. I had just finished one sparkling story concerning the poor little Greek boy and his witty sally ("Piss off!") to the bully-boy tactics of the second cousin of the ex-estate manager of a famous Hollywood beauty whose ex-husband was not known for his heterosexuality. I was about to embark upon another such gem when my dear old friend Lord Whitelaw interrupted me. "Excuse me," he said. "More wine, please, waiter." As I beetled off to the pantry, he then turned to our other friends and, with the impeccable timing of the true aristocrat, said: "Service really isn't what it used to be!" A 24 carat gent through and through as one would expect of an Old Etonian.

There are many tales I could tell about my old buddy Nicholas Soames, the old Harrovian who many are tipping to take over John Major's job soon after Christmas, not all of them printable. One I particularly enjoy is what I said to him after we had an expensive lunch together only a few years ago in the company of a very senior cabinet minister — but my lips are sealed!

Barbara Blancmange, of the luxury dessert dynasty, was kind enough to have me to a dinner given by my old friends Sir Geoffrey and Lady Lockjaw at the Ritz in honour of Sir Jimmy Goldsmith to celebrate making his two hundred and fiftieth million. Jimmy happens to be a very old friend of mine. Barbara gambled that I would be cracking non-stop jokes, and everything did indeed turn out hunky-dory until Lady Annunciata Saveloy, of the snack family, told the whole table that every woman she has ever met has fantasised about having a night of hanky-panky with this poor little Greek boy. I did my best to hide my embarrassment: I haven't received such a compliment since the great

President Nixon himself told my old buddy Soamesy that he'd never received such an efficient shoe-shine. Afterwards I tackled Annunciata in a corridor. Handing her over the agreed sum, I booked her there and then to say the same again at my next dinner, which is being thrown in my honour by yours truly.

In 1974, I had the misfortune to have dinner with Ted Kennedy for the first and only time. It was 1973, and he was the guest of the Greek government. As the guest of the British government, he should have minded his manners, as this was 1976, and a time when manners still meant something. Ted had what those of us who are members of Aspinall's (I was a great friend of Lord Lucan, by the way, and I also once had dinner with Princess Margaret too) call a shaky hold on the truth. Over luncheon that day, he bragged that he had been to bed with hundreds of girls and could beat anyone at tennis. We Greeks are not amused by braggers, particularly when we are infinitely better at tennis than them and have bedded hundreds more girls, but that's the way of the Kennedys. Incidentally, in 1975, I had the misfortune to have dinner with Ted Kennedy for the first and only time when were both guests of the Chilean government. But that, as they say, is another story.

MARGARET THATCHER

THE GRANTHAM YEARS

W e were never idle. There was always work to be done. Rotary, church and shop provided the rhythm of the day. But let no one say we didn't know how to enjoy ourselves. We had studied the matter as a family at length, and, after careful consideration, my father left a good few minutes aside for family leisure activities each year. For five minutes every second Tuesday, we would enjoy ourselves at a session hopping on the spot, with my father shouting out instructions. But we always took care to perform this amusement in different areas of the house, lest it place undue wear and tear on the floorboards. My mother, too, though a serious woman, was full of fun. I remember her smile so well. It came just after 3.00 on June 19th, 1932, though I now forget what prompted it.

W e were Methodists to our bones. The Rev Skinner was a kind and holy man, but misguided in outlook. "Blessed are the poor," he once said, "for theirs is the Kingdom of Heaven". My father took umbrage at this, and with good reason. As a specialist grocer, he understood only too well the need for wealth creation. Such wishy-washy sentiments as the Rev Skinner's would provide little incentive for the less well off, making them a burden to others. The small businessman would suffer disastrously as a consequence. "We must find some way of combining Christian charity with sensible social policy," my father said. "And we can make a good start by giving the poor a short sharp shock." This was the Christian ethic by which I lived my political life. Blessed are the poor, certainly, but only when they become better off.

T here was little time to waste on holidays. Every third year, weather permitting, we would enjoy a morning at Skegness. Up early, my father would set us to work shifting the sand from one end of the beach to the other. It was an uphill task, but we derived enormous satisfaction from it. "Your father always says there's nothing like a tidy beach," declared my mother. After the tide had come in and gone out again, we would set to work with used tissues, drying the entire beach. Four generations of the Roberts family had grown healthy spending their holidays in Skegness in this way. Yet the people of Skegness never took the trouble to thank us for it and it did not surprise me when Skegness voted in a Labour council in 1945. A sentimental attitude towards "welfare" is no substitute for a beach that's spick and span.

My father always said that one can never do without straightforward common sense in matters great as well as small. He never let anyone in his shop who had not first handed over their shoe-laces to my mother at the door. In this way he sought to put an end to petty pilfering. "No one can run far without their shoe-laces," he once said, as an elderly lady plummeted to the floor, a bag of stolen flour bursting beneath her arm. My father was a man of firm principles and a firmer forefinger. Aged ten, I once asked him why, when serving the smoked ham, he always made a point of placing his right forefinger on the weighing scales. He explained it was to give the customers better all-round service, by helping them pay that little bit extra for quality produce. "I always say" he said, "that a finger on the scales is a penny in the till," and I have always treasured this advice.

My mother was quite a saver too. She would encourage us to take long steps whenever walking to chapel so as to save on shoe leather. She once let me in on the secret of how to save money on window cleaners. "Remove all your windows and place them in safe-storage," she advised. "Or better still, lease them out to someone else, thus ensuring an annual profit." She kept the house at North Parade immaculately clean. She achieved this by making my sister wear a feather-duster on her head, and I would be deputed to "wheelbarrow" her around the house every evening. Nowadays, television and radio provide instant entertainment, but I sometimes wonder whether it provides a fraction as much pleasure.

For all our belief in thrift and service, there was always much joy in our home. Every night, my father would let us hear a new saying that he had picked up during the day.

"Watch the pennies," he would say, "and the pounds will look after themselves", or — a personal favourite of his — "Neither a borrower nor a lender be." Then he would throw the topic open to discussion, and the evening would come to a happy conclusion after we had all voiced our agreement. It was from my father that I learnt the value of discussion and consensus. "There's no value in discussion and consensus," he would say. And we agreed.

My grandmother was a cheery soul. Her watchword was fair and immediate punishment for one and all. She would often drop in on our home holding an axe aloft, slamming it blade-down on the table, proclaiming: "The Devil looks after his own" or "Vengeance is Mine saith the Lord", depending on her mood. That may make my grandmother sound rather forbidding. Not at all. She was a kindly woman, often volunteering to come and take her beloved axe to a rat if one was squeaking in the corner near the biscuits. She was also an invaluable asset around the shop. Her father — my great-grandfather — had taught her how to open wooden tea-chests with her teeth. The customers admired her, often lining up and peering through the shop window when she was in residence. Many of them would bear dustbin-lids and pitchforks, just in case. She would fill the house with her laughter, especially after news had come in of a traffic accident, or a natural disaster. Above all, thrift was the quality she instilled in me. On our birthdays, she would award my sister and myself an ice lolly on a stick, but without the cold fruity bit. "Sticks on their own are much better for licking — there's years in them," she would explain. Thus our lollies would last all year, and with excellent savings on dentists' bills to boot. A valuable lesson from my Grantham Years, and one that I have been blessed to suck on ever since.

THE TORY GRANDEES

Paul Johnson: Wherever I go in the world, people stop me in the street, inform me that I'm the one Englishman they still trust, and ask me how we could have got rid of a great leader and replaced her with such a total nonentity. And I hang my head in shame. For I have no answer. How — *HOW* — could they have got rid of Margaret like that? Oh, my God! Have mercy on our souls! Lord, forgive them, for they know not what they do! I'm sorry — sob! — but I can't take it any more.

Sir Peregrine Worsthorne: Chin up, old chap. Borrow my hankie. Good big blow. And another. Wipe it all better. You're quite right, Paul. This present Prime Minister, whatsis name —

Lord Wyatt: Major.

Sir Peregrine Worsthorne: That's the one. Total disaster. He has no sense of history whatsoever. Not like me. The Battle of Hastings — 1066. Spanish Armada — 1588-ish, wasn't it? I'm pretty sure it was. Anyway — Major wouldn't have the foggiest. Not the foggiest. Battle of Bannockburn — 1415. He wouldn't know that. And he's a cad, too. I once sat in the Commons Press Gallery to watch him make an ass of himself at Prime Minister's Questions, and, do you know, he couldn't even be bothered to wave. Cut me dead.

Lord Wyatt: Tosh. John's by far our greatest Prime Minister since — ooh — since the Duke of Wellington. He's done fantastic things for the Tote, for instance, giving it real leadership. And under his premiership, the majority of ordinary decent people in this country are able to live in eight-bedroomed houses in Belgravia.

Kingsley Amis: Bah! I don't like all his Common Market claptrap. I went into a veg shop yesterday, and said "What the hell's that?" and do you know what the man replied? He said, "'Ere, Guv, gorblimey — that's an onion, lorluvaduck". And it was! There are onions everywhere in veg shops these days — and it's all down to some bloody EEC directive. Good god — my wine bottle's finished. They don't make them as big as they used to. Bloody EEC.

Sir Peregrine Worsthorne: Incidentally, what a marvellous ear for the everyday nuances of ordinary people you possess, Kingsley. But there's no getting away from it, Major's a fool and a bounder, and this young fellow Blenkinsop —

Paul Johnson: Blair.

Sir Peregrine Worsthorne: That's the one. Terry Blair. Frankly, I don't like the cut of his jib. Could you really bring yourself to vote for someone who admits to never having worn a bowler hat? I mean, really! And he was once dreadfully rude to me. We were in the same room together — The Wembley Stadium, if memory serves — and I naturally assumed that he would do me the common courtesy of coming over and finding out my views on matters of national and international importance. Yet he never addressed a single word to me, even though we were easily within a hundred yards of one another, with nothing but riff-raff in between. Not one single word. Absolutely cut me dead. I'm sorry, but that's not my idea of how a future Prime Minister should behave.

Paul Johnson: But he's a true patriot, he says his prayers and he brushes his teeth. That's good enough for me. I've spoken to people in the know, and they say he's perfectly ready to step down in favour of Margaret Thatcher the day after he becomes Prime Minister. And as for that Major — I have it on the highest authority that since entering Number 10 he's twice been arrested for shoplifting women's underwear from leading stores, At least that's what the Tories who matter tell me.

Kingsley Amis: Ever since we got into this bloody Common so-called Market, my trousers have been far too tight, especially after lunch. And these damn collars too! No space for your neck! Typical frogs, trying to reduce the size of an Englishman's wardrobe. Bloody disgrace. This claret tastes a bit off. Bah! Someone forgot to put any scotch in it.

Lord Wyatt: But John Major's achievements are legion. He's single-handedly reduced the number of unprofitable patients clogging up our great hospitals. Whenever he goes abroad, he is greeted as an equal by the under-secretaries of state. His charismatic, no-nonsense approach has brought amazing material benefits to the decent working man And I should know — I am that decent working man. Your prejudice against him is entirely based on class snobbery.

Paul Johnson: Rubbish! I know for certain from leading Tories that Major has been secretly diagnosed by leading physicians as a schizophrenic psychopath with paranoid tendencies towards hysteria and megalomania. When he can't force through a decision at cabinet level, he regularly draws out a pistol and opens fire. And his ignorance is as widespread as it is contemptible: he uses his fingers to count, always gets the 'r' in his own name the wrong way round and the book he took with him on his last visit to America was the second — and easiest — in the Ant and Bee series. All that, *and* his secret conviction last year on a charge of heroin smuggling — the fellow's a dolt and a brigand.

Lord Wyatt: That is not the view of the Governor of the Bank of England, Lord Weinstock, the 500 leading chairmen of British Industry, or the Queen.

Paul Johnson: Bah! How do you know?

Lord Wyatt: Because I tell them what to think.

Sir Peregrine Worsthorne: That's not what Lilibet told me last time she dropped round to help with the dishes. Anyway, Major sometimes wears grey socks. No gentleman ever wears grey socks. And rumour has it he didn't even go to public school — and I'm most certainly not being snobbish, Woodrow — just concerned.

Paul Johnson: I don't believe there can be anything fundamentally wrong with this country when four highly civilised people such as ourselves can enjoy a thoroughly good-natured and combative luncheon like this, bartering intellectual cut-and-thrust of the highest calibre over the table. But of course it wouldn't have been possible were it not for Margaret Thatcher, God bless her.

Kingsley Amis: Burp. The Frogs couldn't put on a lunch like this. No sense of humour. Nor could the Krauts. No sense of humour. And as for the Yanks — no sense of humour. Burp. The English are the only people who could fill a table with a gathering of intellectuals like us. We're the creme de la creme. Eh? Eh? Did I hear someone mention a large Creme de Menthe? Burp.

A VIRAGO KEEPSAKE DIARY

Germaine Greer: My God, we needed it. Twenty five years ago, when Virago began, we writing women were crudely and immaturely caricatured as ball-breaking harridans — a prejudice I took pains to refute in a long and considered article for OZ magazine at the time ("Cut Their Balls Off", May 1975).

Since then, we women writers have come far, and we now sing gloriously from the hilltops with one beautiful and unified voice. Except, that is, for some women, who persist in doing us down with their careerist ambition and their big feet and their oh-so-happy family life and their "own thoughts" on this and that and their blind refusal to see someone like, say, Germaine Greer as the leading figure in the past twenty five years of liberation. Still, that's what you get from doing your damnedest, sweating blood and guts for others, and a fat lot of good it's done me. Women! Crikey, the way they persist in thinking for themselves rather than following my clear lead really gets up my nose. But then that's women for you.

Grace Nichols: My voice as a writer has its source very much in the Caribbean, which means that psychically you're connected to the Americas, Africa, Asia and Europe, offering a creatively exciting cross-fertilisation.

In this poem, I deal with my female historical past —the streams of memory of a slave woman, the embodiment of all the women who've gone through that humiliating and brutal experience, whilst echoing too the other sides of my personality — particularly my sense of fun, my powers of observation and my extraordinary compassion for the oppressed:

> *i is a virago author*
> *i is a virago author*
> *i is woman, i is black*
> *mi poems ain't yo poems*
> *but now you bought dem you*
> *   can't take dem back*
> *so dere.*

Elizabeth Wilson: I first met Carmen Callil in I forget which year. At this particular meeting, — was it a meeting? I forget — Carmen, like me, was knitting. Knitting was enjoying a revival, re-evaluated as an underrated women's craft. The year before — or was it the year before that? — those of us at the forefront of the women's movement had experimented with car maintenance, and the year after — or was it the year before the year after? — a breakaway group on the cutting edge of feminism were leading a radical re-appraisal of washing-up, making their own scouring pads in an allwoman co-operative. But at that time — if it was at that time — most of our concerns were echoed in knitting. Many of us saw it as a microcosm of the paradigm that was the encapsulation of the ethos of the energisation of the notion of the value-system of the network of the passionate concerns of our struggle: it was as simple as that.

I had been knitting daily for two years. Click-click, click-click, click-click. For hour upon hour, my needles would click together. But Carmen's first words to me — I'll never forget them — were, "Have you ever tried doing that with wool?"

With those few words, my eyes were opened. Over the two long years in which I had been knitting, I had felt an increasing gap — emotional, sexual, psycho-sociological — that seemed to separate me from the knitting output of other women. Surely, I felt in my bones, there must be more to knitting — more to life — than simply clicking two needles together. Other people — other women — had produced pullovers, scarves, and cardigans, but at the end of two years solid knitting I had managed to produce nothing. Until that moment when Carmen suggested wool.

Unprompted, I went out and bought my first ball of wool on December 31st, 1979. But the very next day, without warning, the Seventies gave way to the Eighties, and a new spirit took over. Somehow the feminism of the 1980s was not conducive to knitting, so I never made my scarf. Instead, I transformed the ball of wool into something more suited to the 80s *zeitgeist*: a single long thread reaching upstairs, ready to ravel or unravel as the mood took me. I wonder if Carmen still knits? Did she ever knit? I forget. I wrote so much in the eighties, perhaps that was my knitting, my books my polo-necks. In my next Virago book, *Women, Wool and The Dichotomy of Labour: The Absolute Knit*, I hope to explore this whole subject — what whole subject? I forget — in even greater depth, if at all.

Maya Angelou: Words. Words. Words. Words.
Words. Words. Words.

That's seven words in all: words, words, words, words, words, words. And words. Seven words, all the same, all "words". And all my children. My own beautiful children, who bring me so much pleasure and delight. Seven words. Or fifty two words now, including these words. But still not quite enough words to get me to the end of this very sacred and precious Keepsake.

Sometimes, interviewers say to me, they say, "Maya Angelou, everyone knows you are one of the greatest writers in this world of ours today. Everyone knows you can make words sing and dance and play so merrily on the page, you can make them waltz around maypoles and throw their hands in the air and catch dollar bills floating through the air in this great big beautiful universe. And everyone knows that the story of your life is a shining beacon to all those folks who wish to grow to be like you. You have done so many things in your life: brave things, noble things, beautiful things, things of genius. But today, Maya Angelou, how would you describe yourself?" This is the sort of question they ask.

And you know what I reply? I reply, "Honey, did you say '*one* of the greatest writers in the world', is that what you said? Because if that's really what you said, I don't think we understand one another, honey, you know really I don't."

And then you know what I say? I say, "As the world's greatest writer, I approach my job with humility. I like to put my trust in words. I am their most humble servant. I wait upon adverbs. I serve candy to pronouns. I press the suits of prepositions. But I won't take no haughty behaviour from no jumped-up two-bit little conjunction, you bet I won't."

How do I write? I place my pen upon the pad and I open my window to allow the great writers of the past to enter into my writing room. Shelley. Gerard Manley Hopkins. Gide. Dorothy Wordsworth. Keats. Christina Rossetti. William Shakespeare. They all parade around the room, whispering to me of their poesy and their prose. And you know what I reply to these great writers? I reply, "Stop your boney chattering and shove off! You're all dead and gone and Maya Angelou, she wants to write!"

Words. Words. Words.
Words. Words.
Words. Words. Words.

MARINA WARNER

I am certainly not advocating the mass destruction of all humankind. Far from it. That would be absurd, and not only absurd but morally reprehensible. In fact, the last thing I want is the mass destruction of all humankind, which to my mind is an over-ridingly 'male' idea. In fact, as novels from Jane Austen's *Emma* to Booker Prize winner Ben Okri's *Famished Road* have demonstrated so tellingly, every male has deep genocidal instincts, apart from those who do not. Rather, I am advocating a profound and important re-evaluation of our cultural and political preconceptions to incorporate the view from my road in Kentish Town, which is surely not too much to ask of anyone.

Never before has society been so indifferent to the pipe. Popeye the Sailor Man* is just one embodiment of male culture that intensifies one's sense of the hero as pipesmoker, another being Sherlock Holmes, and another Sir John Harvey-Jones. Yet, despite all evidence to the contrary, there remains a culture of what one might term sublime apathy in our society towards the pipe. The ex-Prime Minister Harold Wilson was also a keen pipe-smoker, and many leading historians contend that Agamemnon** may well have smoked a pipe before setting off to do battle against Carthage. Many of our most memorable contemporary novels have been written by pipe-smokers — Malcolm Bradbury, Sir William Golding, Keri Hulme — and leading anthropologists have shown that in some African tribal societies the pipe is seen as a potent and living symbol for the reception and smoking of tobacco. In contemporary 'Westerns', native Americans are often portrayed smoking the pipe of peace, and many shops within our contemporary culture — particularly pipe shops — display nothing but pipes in their windows. One of the scientists in Spielberg's *Jurassic Park* smokes a pipe, so does one of the teachers in Roddy Doyle's Booker Prizewinning novel, *Paddy Clarke Ha Ha Ha*, and so too did the famous actor James Robertson Justice in *The Yellow Rolls Royce* * * *

We live in a society — menacing, subdued, hopeful, hopeless, brave, cowardly, fat, thin, hot, cold, big, little — which is gradually awakening with some kind of seeping dread to the fearful dominance of the pipe and the evolving expectations that surround it. In California, two trained scientists**** observed a stationary pipe under clinical conditions. They placed it on a table two metres by two metres, left the room, and, through a peep-hole — *so that it had no idea that it was being observed* — they watched it, around the clock, for a full twenty-three days. Extraordinarily, their records show that, through a remarkable show of sheer willpower, at no time whatsoever did the pipe reveal any sign of movement, or, indeed of comprehension. Only when they removed it from its room, filled it with tobacco, ignited the tobacco, and began to puff did the pipe take on the normal attributes invested in it by society. Small wonder that society is, at the deepest level, so beguiled by this seemingly most innocent yet also most threatening of objects. Already, plaintive, accusatory signs are to be seen in restaurants: "Please refrain from smoking pipes as it may offend other diners". Only when we learn to smoke the pipe can we be sure that it will cease to smoke us. Never before has society been so obsessed with the pipe. Thank you. *****

One of the most potent myths in our hidebound society lies in the overwhelming adulation afforded by the media to the myth of the well-spoken, pretty, soft-left, female, lapsed Catholic middlebrow. She has become as powerful, in her way, as Pegasus, Robocop, Billie Holiday or Kaspar Hauser, appearing at least once an hour on television and radio, perhaps because she offers to the producers a blueprint of idealised human nature, and, at a deeper, psychic level, instils in them a sort of deep reassurance, as she is freely available to hold forth on any topic at the drop of a hat without any form of "meaning" to get in the way******

John Lennon, Pericles, Song Lines, Clarissa, The Ozone Layer, Weston-Super-Mare, Dave Lee Travis, Gustav Holst, Mary Poppins, Dr Johnson, The Faerie Queene, Watergate, Colin Macinnes, The Home Improvements Act 1987. Rumpelstiltskin. The Berlin Wall, Stockhausen, The Virgin Mary, AIDS, Mahatma Gandhi, All Gas and Gaiters, The Beveridge Report, The Ring Cycle, Ring Around the Moon, Ring Lardner, Give Us A Ring, Goering, Gowing, Gonne — these topics, unrelated in so many ways, are in fact linked by one extraordinary, telling and ultimately overriding pertinent fact: I have just gathered them all in a single sentence, becoming, in all modesty, arguably the first woman in history ever so to do.

see "Olive Oyl: Myth, Function and Reality" M. Warner, New Statesman, 6.10.72
** *see "Memnons Aga: Stylish Yet So Very User-Friendly", M. Warner, Food and Drink Magazine, 19.12.92.*
*** *see "Yellow Cars in the Movies of the 50's and the Growth of a Pluralistic Society" M. Warner, Sight and Sound, 4.5.89.*
**** *see "The Perennial Use Of Made-Up Scientists To Prop Up A Specious Argument and*

Other Essays" M. Warner, Parrot Press, 16.4.84.
***** *see "Footnotes Do Furnish an Essay" M. Warner, Interiors magazine, 13.8.88.*
****** *for a more detailed account, see M. Warner's 5th Reith Lecture, "Marina: Myths Mythmanaged and Mythtaken".*

These We Have Loved

DENNIS POTTER

The sight of a fresh spring daffodil bursting forth into the dappled sunlight fills me with disgust and despair. What sort of a world have we created for ourselves that allows these yellowy, sickly, foul-smelling, so-called "flowers" to shove their misshapen and elongated necks through the Lord's earth and then lets their vomit-coloured petals infringe the sanctity of our own old and very dear English countryside? What have we as a nation in, I fear, a deep and irreversible decline, busily wallowing in our post-colonial cowardice. puffing our chest up and then wheezing like some bronchial old colonel, what have we as a nation come to when we allow these daffodils, these malevolent globules of terminal jaundice, all yellow, yellow, yellow, to poke their noses through *our* ground and into *our* private lives?

I come up with a smashing new idea for a revolutionary drama series. There's this girl, naked but for her crotchless panties, and she may or may not be a symbol of Britain in decline, and then there's this man ill in bed who experiences flashbacks to a blind girl who may or may not have been raped by the devil at a middle-class dinner party in the Fifties. Then suddenly they all start miming:

"Sugar! Ooh, Honey Honey!
You are my candy girl
And you got me wantin' you
Oh, Sugar! Ooh Honey Honey!'
while the naked girl offers them a cake shaped like a phallus. British TV won't have seen anything like it ever before. Any takers?

LORD
WEIDENFELD

Last month saw the publication of my autobiography, *Remaindering My Good Friends* (£20.00), in which I lay to rest many myths about myself, among them that the books I publish invariably contain too many mispronts. Frankly, nothing could be further from the tooth. Also, my good friends Henry Kissinger, the Longfords, David Owen, Isaiah Berlin, the Sieffs, the Gettys, the Kennedys, President Bush and the Rothermeres have all informed me, at one time or another, that some people have accused me of social-climbing. These accusations, too, are inspired by alice. I need hardly say that, given the choice of a dustman or a duke, I would as soon talk to a dustman as to a duck.

It was at a delightful party thrown by the influential, outgoing and charming Brooke Astor for Mrs Mildred 'Puffy' Hillman, the prominent Isle of Man political hostess, to introduce the outgoing, charming and influential property magnate Eddie 'Kneecapper' Malone to the various strands — intellectual, political, social — of Milwaukee society that I first met the charming, influential and outgoing Lady Sophie Money-Bagges. I recognised at once that she was not only attractive and intelligent, but that she had a hoard of gold. "You must ride a cook for us," I said to her over dinner, and eight years later I was proud to publish her autobiography, *A Life of My Onw* (12pp) in a specially limited edition of three, two of which she kept for herself, and one of which she was permitted to give, after tough negotiating on my part, to her sister.

Lady Sophie was a woman of simple tastes; this was reflected in the way she decorated her various houses in Gstaad, London, Washington, Venice, Aspen, Stockholm and New York. She would always insist that each window be hung with only one set of curtains, that guests should perform their own morning ablutions and that after every dinner party the best plates, dishes, bowls and saucers should be cleaned for further use the next day rather than simply be thrown away. In every way, Sophie was harm itself. Regrettably I have seen little of her since her ill-fated bankruptcy; but then the outskirts of Bradford have always been so much harder to get to than the slopes of Gstaad.

In the course of my life, I have published many a distinguished title, some of whom have managed to write perfectly reasonable books. Works I remember with particular affection include [MEMO: LOOK UP APPROPRIATE NAMES AND INSERT]. Many people have asked me what my secret is. Frankly, at dinners such as those given by my good friends the talented, self-effacing and witty yet considerate Giovanni Agnellis, I like to commission a book from whomsoever I am placed next to. It is a great ice-breaker, and in my early years this method resulted in the publication of such notable works as *My Life As An Under-cook, How to Be a Successful Doorman* and *A Chauffeur Remembers.*

Later, I mixed in the very top circles, for many years helping the then Prime Minister, the beautiful, elegant and effervescent Harold Wilson in his onerous task of ruining the country.

I will never forget my Downing Street Years. Often, having popped into the Number 10 sitting room, one would find oneself surrounded by the 'great and the good', all working flat out to make Britain a better place to lift in. In one corner, Marcia would be hard at work, felt-tip in hand, tackling the extensive Wilson flies, while over in the other corner Arnold Goodman, Joseph Kagan and Eric Miller would be on their knees designing appropriately tasteful coats of arms for themselves and their close friends and political clients.

A lot of nonsense — much of it spiteful — has been written about the so-called 'Lavender List' of those deemed worthy of inclusion in Wilson's Resignation Honours. Yet Harold's sole intention was to pay tribute to those of us who had swerved our country. Now that the fuss has died down, it seems clear to most reasonable people that Sir Reginald Kray, Lord Biggs, Lord Savundra, Sir James Goldsmith and Lord Khashoggi were wholly deserting of such honours.

How should one describe Wilson? For all his intellectual brilliance, he had an understated elegance about him combined with an outgoing charm which made him ideally suited to the job. Lady Falkender, too, was a formidable character: for all her intellectual brilliance, she had an understated elegance about her combined with an outgoing charm which made her ideally suited to the job. As to Harold's wife Mary, I would say that for all her intellectual brilliance, she had an understated elegance about her combined with an outgoing charm which made her ideally suited to the job. Three very different characters, their idiosyncrasies brought to life, I trust, by these brief 'pen-portraits'.

It was at a highly congenial party thrown by Drue Heinz for Mrs Oatsy Leiter to celebrate Marietta Tree's reception for Eppi Evron's dinner for Drue Heinz that I first commissioned a twenty-volume history of the brain from Professor Gropius. Regrettably, a misprint must have crept into our conversation for the full manuscript of a substantially different work *A Twenty Volume History of the Bra* arrived on my desk ten years later. Thankfully, our decision to publish it as an art-book of a superior kind with a foreword by the talented, beautiful and self-assured Lady Antonia Fraser met with great success. At a party thrown by Drue Heinz to celebrate publication, I suggested to the Professor that he should tackle my original proposal. I am delighted to announce that *A Twenty Volume History of the Rain* is to be published next month.

Christmas has just been, and as usual we put out the decorations. I am afraid to say that when I came to inspect the crib, I found that my wife had got into a dreadful muddle, placing the Three Kings with their luxury goods and words of great wisdom outside the modest but comfortable lodgings. Inside, she was giving pride of place to a bearded young man, an unmarried mother, their toddler and a group of farm labourers. "I have heard of the spirit of Christmas, but this is ridiculous!" I exclaimed, moving the Three Kings into the warmth and placing all the others out of sight under the carpet. "My dears, you simply must write a book for us!" I said to the Three Kings when they had a minute, hinting that I might attempt to negotiate a foreword from His Royal Highness King Herod.

VIVIENNE WESTWOOD OBE

I love books and not only that but I thoroughly enjoy them, and when I can find the time I especially like reading them all the way through, with or without pictures, the older the better. That Michael Proust was such a clever man, don't you think. What was it he said about temps? That's it — he said he was "in search of temps perdu" which of course literally translated from the Italian means "in search of lost temps". Just imagine it, there he was, up to his neck in this great big book, this massive *oeuf*, as he would have called it, and the temps hadn't even bothered to show up. Poor lamb. I'm thinking of calling my next collection, "In the Footsteps of Michael Proust" in his honour, with all these beautiful girls dressed in the temp style, with little shorthand pads sewn into their noses, and fantastic six-inch platform heels shaped like typewriters. We need revolutions like that, because to my mind that's the only way that Britain will come to its senses and transform itself into a wholly cultural society, along the lines suggested by Bernard Russell, the great philatelist. Have you read him? Oh, but you *must*. His tailoring was always *impeccable*.

As Degas once said to Mallarmy: "Hello Mallarmy, my name is Degas." I myself have the very deepest respect for Degas, I'm a real Degas digger, you might say, and several of his poems have inspired my most recent Vivienne Westwood collection, "It's Amazing But I Really Can't Stop Having Great Big Thoughts", which many people in the fashion world are already describing, perhaps a little grudgingly, as the greatest work so far by one of the greatest fashion geniuses of the 20th century, namely myself.

The centrepiece is my famous "Heart of Darkness" range, inspired by the seafaring novels of Joseph Conrad such as *Lord John* and *Typhoo*. It takes the umbrella as its main motif, because in those days it could be absolutely pelting at sea, and there's umbrellas on the lapels of all my jackets and umbrellas on the breast of all my T-shirts. And of course all my lovely girl models wore Conrad-style bushy beards and sou'westers when they were modelling my acclaimed Conrad Corset Collection. And I discovered over the course of my lengthy historical research at the Victoria and Edward Museum that in those days seafarers who were taking produce from England to Borneo via the highly treacherous Menai Straits found platform heels generally got in the way, so in the interests of accuracy my evening range of Conradish long dresses is now teamed with wellington boots, with waders for morning wear.

I sometimes wonder whether I can halt it all by myself. The stagnation of Western culture in the 20th century, I mean. What was it La Rouchefoucoff once said? I forget.

Back in that amazing summer of '77, with my invention of the punk, I singlehandedly changed society for ever, bringing down the iron rule of the repressive Tory government under Mrs Thatcher, opening up a new and exciting error — the Eighties — in which people from all walks of life could come off the streets into my shops and really express their freedom and their contempt for Western materialism and their own incredible individuality by buying my range of exotic safety-pin leisurewear in a choice of two colours for just £1250 plus VAT, with an option of pocket-flaps for an additional £75 plus VAT, perhaps with an ironic Westwood LET'S SET FIRE TO SOCIETY hat shaped like an ironic crown for an ironic £199 plus VAT.

I hate it when people say "It's only fashion", really hate it. "What do you mean, 'It's only fashion'?" I reply. As A J Air once said, "Purple See-Through Jump-Suits are all about Language, Truth and Logic", but of course it's only those last four words that are ever remembered. To me, fashion is intrinsically concerned with morality and politics and changing society and the evidence for this is obvious if you know your history. For instance, some of you may already know that the French Revolution occurred in 1789. But how many of you knew that at the end of the previous year a revolutionary new type of black tulle corset with floral imprints had become widely available in the Paris fashion salons? In the same way, the downfall of President Nixon came in 1974, the very same year in which the Tank-Top took America by storm. Let's look at some other more major historical events, forged by my direct influence as a fashion designer:

1978: The Vivienne Westwood Paris collection displays for the very first time my revolutionary pink stretch velour shoulder seams on a crenellated pinafore-style rubber bustier embroidered with fin-de-siecle Beardsley-style handstitched prints. Less than six weeks later, the Shah of Iran is driven into exile by supporters of the Ayatollah and the Islamic revolution has begun.

1982: I exclusively reveal my velvet Tudor bloomers with appliqué stitching in bright orange, purple and mauve. General Galtieri invades the Falkland Islands. In an unexpected move, I bring forward my new collection of Diane Arbus-inspired straitjacket undergarments for an immediate launch. On June 14th, 1982, the Argentinians surrender

1989: My outrageous bondage-style evening wear collection, "I Think Therefore I Is", with safety-pin style navel decoration accessories and matching earrings, is launched in London to universal acclaim. Overnight, the Berlin Wall comes down.

1994: I attract worldwide attention and acclaim when I appear in a see-through evening dress to dinner at Kensington Palace. Just six weeks later, Nelson Mandela is elected President of South Africa in the first-ever democratic elections in that divided country. And yet still they continue to say: "It's only fashion."

People often ask me, just as they must have asked Aldous Hucksley and before him Norman Mainer: "Vivienne, from whence hails your fantastic inspiration?" "From all around me," is the answer. Just this morning, I saw a milk bottle on a doorstep. By noon I was already planning the Vivienne Westwood John Stewart Mill Gold Top Collection for next Spring, with fifteen beautiful models all entering in a fantasy milk float, wearing milk bottle platform heels, bustiers made from cherry yoghurt cartons and skirts created from all the separate slices you find in a loaf of readysliced bread, all beautifully stitched together by hand. At just £1950 plus VAT, it's going to start a new cultural revolution at the street level, and by the end of the year the Tories will be on the run. Now, remind me, love, what was it Wittgenstein said about Hot Pants?

MICHAEL WINNER

The other night I dined in the Cafe Royal. Personally, I found the atmosphere rather tepid. It was all right when I came in, with hundreds of people — none famous — yacking away. But straightaway there was silence and within minutes they had all cleared out, leaving me all by myself. This happens everywhere I go these days. What on earth have British restaurants come to?

"Do you know who I am?" That's a question that brings them up pretty smartly, I can tell you.

The last time I spent £1200 on a light lunch at The Savoy was back in 1973, when spending £1200 on lunch really meant something. It was a jolly nice lunch in the company of my very good friends who know and like me a lot and are happy to count themselves the very good friends of Michael Winner, and now I'm talking about stars of the calibre of Paul Daniels, Roger Tonge of *Crossroads* fame, Popeye the Sailor Man, and Clarence the Cross-Eyed Lion of *Daktari* fame, my very very good friend Ursula Andress having rung through at the last moment with her apologies, too bad.

This time things weren't so good. In fact, they were bloody awful. When I arrived, the ghastly young man on the front desk threw me a curt, "Good morning, sir, how can I help you?" to which, quick as a flash, I replied, "Do you know who I am — I'm Michael Winner and I demand the best, so less of the good morning sirs and more of the service! Is our table ready yet?"

"Have you booked, sir?" he replied

smugly. Rarely have I been so insulted. Whatever happened to old-fashioned manners while we're about it? "Of course I haven't booked, you prat. How dare you! I demand to see the manager. Do you know who I am?"

When finally the manager deigned to arrive, a full two minutes and fifteen seconds later, I was perfectly straightforward and helpful, unloosening my own belt and removing my trousers and Y-fronts. "Can I help at all, sir?" he said.

"You certainly can," I replied, leaning over, "I would like my arse licked."

"I'm afraid, sir, that is not a service we can provide," he replied.

So much for the customer, I thought.

"Then I will take my custom elsewhere," I replied. "Come on, Sarah, we're off."

And with that I exited — leaving one very disappointed hotel behind me. Now they'll never be able to boast they once served the director of *Kill, Kill and Kill Again 2* — that'll teach them to be so snooty!

For my annual birthday lunch at The Connaught, I booked the best table in the house with a dozen seats and invited a number of my world-famous celebrity friends, all of them very rich indeed as well as being very famous, and rich with it, and incidentally great friends of mine, and world-famous too.

After I had been sitting there for an hour, I waved my napkin at the awful head waiter, who came rushing. "Do you know who I am?" I said. "So, what's the meaning of this, then, you loathsome creature?"

If you can believe it, the stupid oaf pretended not to understand. So I spelt it out in words of one syllabubble.

"You've FORGOTTEN THE TELEVISION!" I said. I sensed that admiring glances were being aimed in my direction from diners on all the surrounding tables. "Are you honestly expecting me to eat a highly expensive meal in a so-called five star establishment without a television to watch! I ask you!"

As the ageing crone rushed away for a telly, I turned to my great friends, among them Marlon Brando and Sean Connery and Raquel Welch and Sophia Loren and cast my eyes to the ceiling.

"Excuse me, sir." It was a young and obviously thoroughly inexperienced waiter.

"Yes?"

"Would you like me to clear these places away? Your guests don't seem to be coming."

"What do you mean — don't seem to be coming! What nonsense!" I said, looking round at the chairs. "They're Hollywood's finest superstars, my lad, and they're my greatest friends, and they're all here with me now —and don't you ever suggest that they're not! More Chateau Latour, Marlon, love?"

That showed him! And my brave outburst had the salutary effect of making the stuck-up Connaught eat humble pie because when the bill came they'd only charged me for one, letting in all my great friends for nothing! One thing's for sure — they obviously know who I am!

W hat sickens me about today's society is that ordinary men and women live in daily fear of getting mugged, raped or shot in the street. My own varied range of first-rate action movies, which includes *Death Wish 1*, in which a buxom young lady without a brassiere is mugged and then raped, *Death Wish 2*, in which a buxom young lady without a brassiere is mugged and then raped, *Death Wish 3*, in which a buxom young lady without a brassiere is mugged and then raped, *Death Wish 4*, in which a buxom young lady without a brassiere is mugged and then raped and, of course, the innovative *Death Wish 5* in which the buxom young lady without the brassiere is first raped and then mugged, have made it clear that violence in a decent society is to be totally abhorred. When will these thugs start listening to the voice of sanity?

P icasso, Braque and I have all, at one time or another, eaten at the Colombe D'Or. I took Sarah along there for dinner in my chauffeur-driven Rolls. Perusing the menu, I said to her: "Jenny, my dear, you may choose whatever you want from the set menu, whilst I myself will investigate the à la carte, Mandy, my love." So the delicious young lady in question dutifully put down her magazine and stared at the menu.

Frankly, service was a bit slow, so I took out my chain-saw and carved up the table. I need hardly add that the delectable young lady at the next table was positively delighted by the performance, holding her hands to her lovely young cheeks and screaming seductively. And then it struck me. Looking out the window, there was no view. Typical! I picked up my megaphone and called the manager.

"What eez ze trouble, m'sieur?" he said, in a horrible accent, French no doubt.

"There's no view!" I said.

"But it eez night-time, m'sieur", he replied. "It eez peetch dark."

"So this is what eating out in France has come to?! No view at night-time!" I said. "I mean, how much do you have to pay for a decent view these days? Let's go, Samantha! I'm certainly never coming back here again. Do you know who I am?"

JEANETTE WINTERSON

As a woman, as a working class woman, one is a robber, a pirate, a brigand sailing dangerous waters. One doesn't belong in safe society, one is beyond the pale, a vagrant, a scoundrel, a fishmonger, a rapscallion, a popinjay, a poltroon, a pantechnicon. So I'm in the vanguard of a different kind of writing, a writing that will one day rise up and scythe through that middle-class complacency, that cottonwool world of male writers, writers with hoses dangling from their legs like petrol pumps, with four stars branded upon their clavicembalos in scarecrow red. At the moment, I'm by myself, a lone voice in the wilderness, crying and singing and bleating and wailing (but not whaling) against the massed armies of the middle-class male, so I stand rejected and sore and shivering in the brimey cold of rejection within a London ravaged and ravaged again and again and again and again, with gruesome repetitiveness, by the Thatcher beast with her strap-on monetarism.

And I howl for love.

And I howl for art.

And I howl for social justice.

And I howl in my heroic isolation.

And I howl for some halfway decent tea for a change, how about some Fortnum's Earl Grey, honestly you employ a cook and a cleaning lady and a driver and a whole raft of secretaries and the best they can come up with is crappy PG Tips, I'll smash their faces, it makes me hopping

Mad.

What are you that makes me feel thus? Are you thus what makes me feel that? Feel me thus that you makes what are? You are my winged Pegasus, my hirsute daffodil, my sea urchin of song, my orang-utan pirouetting on a high wire, my banana unpeeled, my mango spurting vertiginous aspidistras over the umbrous concavities of Sappho's juts and nooks. You affect me as a young gazelle affects the mountain over which it lollops, dollops and, er, sollops — oh, bollops.

I close my beautiful brown deep brown soft brown eyes. My lips like smoked salmon wrapped in cream cheese parcels with a sprig of fennel, moist, urgent, costly but on special offer, meet your lips, as fresh and nutritious as the morning's cod. My tongue laps your lips; your lips are lapped, and, lapping lips lip lappingly like lollipops over lipped laps slapped slippingly. Your mouth opens and closes, blowing and sucking, sucking and blowing as my hands wreath your gills in luscious circles of contentment. Your gills? Wreathe your gills? I open my eyes. My God! It is not you at all, but the goldfish I am kissing! That which I am kissing is the goldfish! Who put the goldfish bowl by my bloody desk? You'll pay for this, you will! Will you this for pay you'll!

What is love? Love belongs to itself, deaf to pleading and unmoved by violence. No one can legislate love; it cannot be given orders or cajoled into service. Love is a clear pool. Love is a sunlit sky. Love is a bird in flight. Love means never having to say you're sorry.

My own love for mankind is unfettered and unfounded, a boulder set adrift in a sea of indifference. I love human beings with a love inexorable and incurable, ineluctable and inseparable, like the love of a toenail for its toe, or a sausage — so sage — for its skin. My love is a love for all human beings, for their grain and ebb, for their woof and pelmet, for their sob and trill, for their sock and espadrille, a love unfettered by the value placed on it by the nauseating Thatcherite market economy. My love is a love for all human beings, every single one, unique in their uniqueness. Except for men, of course. And old women, their skins parched and yellow like discarded phonebooks. And futile heterosexual women, prepared every day, every hour, every minute, to act as the cake into which man's knife must plunge. And subservient lesbian women, drifting like zombies as the handmaidens to the words of one so much braver and more passionate and more alive than themselves. Yes — my love is a love for all human beings, save all those who are not myself.

My reading for the beach (be, ache) this summer? My new book has been described by no less a writer than Jeanette Winterson as "a rich book, bawdy and beautiful, shocking *because* of its beauty, an antidote to the numbness of modern life. A dangerous book, banked with ideas forced out of the words themselves, not words for things, but words that are living things with the power to move, not move in the sense of move, exactly, but move in the sense of move, you know, so that in the end you feel as though something must be done about it all, and that it's worth moving if you can't stay still." So I will most certainly be taking that one. I am also planning to re-read all the earlier works of Jeanette Winterson, which have been described by Jeanette Winterson, the only contemporary critic, in the opinion of the profoundly wise Jeanette Winterson, who has any form of serious critical engagement, as "among the few books written this century worthy to be placed alongside the collected works of Jeanette Winterson". A must.

Fifteen years of the gunboated gumbooted hand of Conservative government has made everyone — the executive zombies, the shop zombies, the writerly zombies, the zombie zombies — more self-centred. Oh, see them as they sit in their expensive mansions doodling in delight, looking down on the teeming, toiling, millions, minions! See them as they create their dark factories of slaves in basements working for them, night and day, day and night, and afternoons and mornings too. Hark as they gratingly glory in their own market value, sweltering amidst the luxury of furnishings and the furnishings of luxury, happy to let others sweat and toil so that they may be content in the fetid atmosphere of their own self adulation!

Happily, I have managed to create for myself and others an oasis of generosity and unselfishness, set way apart from such egotistical capitalist cravings, a beautiful home where my women friends and my lover and everybody else who works for me in the basement are free in their allotted time to really believe in what I do, and are released by me into an environment where they are enabled to liberate themselves into serving me throughout the day to the best of their abilities, allowing me to express myself, on their behalf, against the tyrannies of the age. Was ever a writer so powerful, so responsible, so poetic, so caring, so *selfless*?

FIN

KEITH RICHARDS' LAST WORDS

What a drag it is movin' house, and all that shit. Like, each time I buy a house — great fucking huge Tudor thing in miles of acres or whatever — I like it for a day or two, even a month maybe — but then I nearly always find there's somethin' wrong with the bathroom. Like, this is wot happened in the first half of last year, maaan:

February: Buy new fuckin' house for a load of bread, but at least it has a brilliant swimming pool for the car.

March: Find corpse of chick in bathroom. Real downer. Sell house.

April: Buy new house wiv luvvly clean bathrooms. Build new upstairs room for throwin' tellies out of.

May: Find corpse in upstairs guest bathroom. Freak out. Dragsville. Sell house.

June: Buy new house. Find it's in France. "But I said I wanted fuckin' Italy this time," I say. "Sorry Keef," they say. "You should speak more clearly." Sell it via *Country Life*, slogan: "No Corpses in Any of the Fuckin' Upstairs Bathrooms".

July: Prospective buyer turns up, zonks around the house, comes back complainin' he's found a corpse in a downstairs bathroom. "I never said nuffink about the DOWNSTAIRS bathrooms," I say, "Don't be so fuckin' choosy, maaan."

The Sixties — they seem like years ago, right? Years and years and years and years ago. Like literally ten years or even longer, right? But I remember them like they were yesterday, which was a Thursday, or was it a Monday? Can't remember. Tuesday — that's it. Or Sunday. Yesterday? Don't talk to me about yesterday — I'm not into the whole tomorrow thing.

Kids these days don't know the meaning of the word "thing". Like, to them it's just a thing. I mean, how many of them have ever swum in a swimming pool without any water in it? We did that all the time in the Sixties, the whole breast-stroke-on-concrete rap, the whole dive-and-smash-your-head-in thing. And how many of them could put their hand on their thing and tell me like they've ever driven a car completely out of their heads into a solid brick wall just to get the fuckin' cigarette fighter to pop out? Nah — they haven't lived, maan, haven't even lived.

Rock 'n'roll, maaan! This morning, or was it last night?, I got this incredible riff in my head:

> Nyah nyah nyah nyah
> Nyah nyah nyah nyah
> Nyah nyah nyah nyah
> Nyah nyah nyah nyah

and then the chorus goes:

> Nyah nyah nyah nyah
> Nyah nyah nyah nyah
> Nyah nyah nyah nyah
> Nyah nyah —nyah

with that last line having a bit of totally unexpected variation in it, know what I mean? Anyway, Mick woz really into it, like completely out of his head with it, and he said it's like a major new development for the band, fuckin' revolutionary, maan, leaving that third

> *nyah*

out of the very last line. So I said, Jeezuz, maaan, I've just had the most amazin' idea let's go one step bloody further, let's really kick shit, let's take another

> *nyah*

out, so the last line ends up:

> *Nyah — — nyah.*

But Mick has a think about it and he says, nope, Keef, we gotta carry the audience wiv us, like, we don't wanna *lose* them, maan, that'd be just too ahead of its time, maybe in five years, so I say, yeah, maybe you're right, Mick, howsabout another bottle of Jack Daniel's, maaan?